4/18/09

To Josh

Love somebody!

[illegible]

"Mr. McClellan masterfully illustrates the importance of intellectual, vocational, and political diversity within the Black community as well as the necessity of moving beyond the racism game....tremendous testimony to his belief in the unlimited potential of Blacks when the invisible shackles of 'The Man' have been broken."
Denise Hooks-Anderson, MD
President, Wellness Healthcare Associates

"A Love Letter to Black People" is not just a call for change in Black self perception. It is a roadmap to that change... Brian McClellan's uses positive landmarks of Black history to open our eyes to our own prejudgments of ourselves... prejudices that block the road toward a natural Black unity of enduring and personal self love. No platitudes. No easy answers. And no excuses for failure. Read this book and then pass it forward!"
Valetta Anderson
Playwright
Resident Teaching Artist at Atlanta's Alliance Theatre

"A Love Letter to Black People is a healing and inspiring education to all of us. The prayer that our hearts and minds may dwell in a place of love and respect for ourselves and our communities resonates in McClellan's words. I think we've all heard before that the Black community must be accountable and responsible, but the one thing that McClellan points out, and that most omit, is that we must first and foremost love. And, from this love all of our dreams shall come true."
Lisa Fritsch
Talk Show Host and Writer

"A Love Letter to Black People" presents hopeful thoughts on race and success to help provide mental empowerment to Black people to overcome any adverse challenge and to take control of their destiny to achieve success both individually and as a community."
Daniel Laroche MD
President Empire State Medical Association

"From beginning to end, "Love Letter" is captivating, insightful, and empowering - a 'must read' for all Americans who want for progressive change in the African-American community."
N. Lynnette McNeely
Past-President, 2008-09, Wisconsin Association of
African-American Lawyers

"This book is thought-provoking. Whether or not you agree with all of the concepts expressed in the book, the notion that one should strive for success in spite of adversity is a most valuable concept; one that we all should strive to follow. The positive growth of our community very likely depends upon it!"
Jean-Pierre Francillette, Esq.
President, Wiley W. Manuel Bar Association
of Sacramento County (2007, 2008)

"Brought about by the need for a concise and relevant outlook on the Black race at this defining moment in our history, Brian McClellan has dealt head-on with issues swept under the rug for far too long. Brian, you are on time and on target."
Chief Andrew Smalling
President, National Organization of Black Law Enforcement Executives (NOBLE) – South Florida Chapter

"This book is a must read for anyone who loves Black people and wants to see us do better. It is beautifully written and will enthrall you from the beginning to the end. It will inform you and inspire you. It will even make you laugh at times such as when Brian writes about the silly reasons we pull someone's 'Black card.'"
Felicia Kemp
Georgia District Governor for Toastmasters International, 2005-2006

"Brian McClellan is head over heels in love! In "A Love Letter to Black People", Brian poignantly expresses this love in a heartfelt conversation with the reader that reflects his deep adoration for the Black community and his commitment to social uplifting. …a passionate plea for individual responsibility infused with audaciously hopeful words of encouragement and inspiration. Read this book and you cannot help but fall in love too!"
John "Jay" Weaver
Founder, StriversRow.com

A Love Letter to Black People

A LOVE LETTER TO BLACK PEOPLE: AUDACIOUSLY HOPEFUL THOUGHTS ON RACE AND SUCCESS
Published by Sherian Publishing

Sherian Publishing
2700 Braselton Highway, Suite 10-390
Dacula, GA 30019–3207

To order additional copies, please contact Sherian Publishing at
www.sherianinc.com
1-888-276-6730

Cover layout by Gary Unger

Printed in the United States of America

Publisher's Cataloging-in-Publication
(Provided by Quality Books, Inc.)

McClellan, Brian.
A Love Letter to Black People: Audaciously Hopeful Thoughts on Race and Success / by Brian McClellan.
p. cm.
LCCN 2008906862
ISBN-13: 978-0-9795676-5-0
ISBN-10: 0-9795676-5-3

1. African Americans--Psychology. 2. African Americans--Race identity. 3. African Americans--Attitudes. 4. Success. 5. Self-actualization (Psychology) I. Title.

E185.625.M33 2009   305.896'073   QBI08-600227

A Love Letter to Black People

Audaciously Hopeful Thoughts on Race and Success

Brian McClellan

S

Atlanta

TABLE OF CONTENTS

ABOUT THE AUTHOR

Brian McClellan will make you say BAM! He is the CEO of BAMSTRONG Presentations, a public speaking and career development firm. His first book, *The Real Bling: How to Get the Only Thing You Need,* is a powerful and critically acclaimed guide to personal and professional development. Prior to becoming an entrepreneur, Brian served as an executive sales leader with Fortune 500 companies Honeywell International and Georgia-Pacific Corporation. He is a graduate of Princeton University and the Columbia Business School.

Brian is a powerful motivational speaker who inspires audiences large and small on the topics of leadership, diversity, and personal and professional development. He is the 2007 and 2008 Toastmasters Georgia State Champion of Public Speaking. Brian also placed in the Top 20 of 30,000 contestants and 225,000 Toastmasters members worldwide in the 2008 Toastmasters International Speech contest.

Brian lives in the Atlanta, Georgia, area with his wife, Sherri, and their two children, Marcus and Gigi.

For more about Brian, please visit
www.bamstrong.com

ACKNOWLEDGEMENTS

To Sherri, Marcus & Gigi: You teach me how to be a better father and a better man every day. I am thankful to have you in my life and I dedicate every day to making sure you feel the same way. I love you.

To My Parents: I can never thank you enough for the role you have played in making me the person I am. However, I will always try to do so by making you proud. I love you.

To Benevolent Others: I am thankful to have "an army" of people in my life who want me to do well. There have been many times when your kind words were just the encouragement I needed to continue to chase my dreams. Thank you for your love.

The "YSBs": I surveyed or interviewed more than one hundred young, successful Black people, or "YSBs," who offered powerful insight regarding how we can love ourselves and our community to greatness. I am truly grateful for your support of *Love Letter* and, more importantly, for providing us examples of Black success, which we can all proudly celebrate and emulate. The "YSBs" who were quoted directly in the Love Letter are listed on the following page as "Quoted Contributors."

QUOTED CONTRIBUTORS

Abdul-Nasim, Nasiba
Anderson, Gina
Andrews, Daniel
Baltimore, Patrice
Beard, Tangela
Blount, Shani
Boudreaux, Bernadette
Breen, Candace
Brown, Edward III
Bush, Candace
Butts, Tim
Caine, Joyce
Canopii, Michele
Celistan, Dwayne
Chavous, Tracey
Collier, Earsell
Coley, Forrest
Crenshaw, Melvin
Downing, Fred
Doyle, Lucretia
Duncan, Crystal
Ellis, Torin
Evans, Lawrence
Gray, Tracy
Golden, Rod
Henry, Renea
Hines, Twanna A.
James, John
Jones, Dwight
Jones, Janel
Jones, Marc
Jones, Oscar
Kirby, Monique
Lewis, Mildred
Lofton, Kathy O.
Miranda, Mark
Proctor, Shonika
Reynolds, John
Robinson, Antonia
Saunders, Natascha
Shellman, Therone
Smith, James
Slayton, Eddie
Stephens, Nichelle
Taylor-Peay, Dwight
Walker, Selvin
Welch, Tammy
Whitfield, Theresa
Williams, Kendall
Williams, Kevin
Williams, Marvin
Wood, Monica
Woods, Shalom
Woodruff, Carmen

INTRODUCTION
IGNORE THE EVIDENCE

Ignore the evidence. If I know one thing about the pursuit of success, it is this. If you want to have any success, you must ignore the evidence. The people who achieve the most do so by ignoring all the reasons why they should not or will not be successful. They ignore the evidence because relying on this "evidence" will cause them to fail. This is especially true for Black people. For Black people, the evidence points to the unavoidable conclusion that being Black is hard and being Black and successful is harder still. Black people, ignore the evidence!

But haven't we been taught that ignoring this sort of evidence can be dangerous, even fatal? And hasn't it, in fact, been fatal for so many of us? Isn't living Black in America without keeping a constant watch for the dangers of being Black in America tantamount to reckless endangerment? Many Blacks would argue that averting one's gaze from racism is just as dangerous as drinking and driving. Either one will get you killed. This is what we have been taught, and yet the future success, perhaps the future survival, of the Black community depends upon our ability to ignore the evidence. But what are we to believe if not our eyes?

To paraphrase Black author and talk show host Tavis Smiley, there is one thing that I know for sure. The people who achieve the greatest success, regardless of race, trust one set of eyes above all others, the eyes in their minds. With these eyes, they see nothing but abundance, greatness upon greatness, and no obstacles that cannot be overcome. Four decades ago, a great man told us he could see clearly from a "mountaintop" that we as a people had not yet scaled. Today, another would-be great man is on the precipice of removing the fog from our downhill view. We as a people will be able to see all of our "mountaintops" and "dreams" more clearly when we start to look past that pesky evidence by which we are so often confronted.

May I remind you that we have seen this movie before? The only reason we Blacks are here today is because Blacks who came before us ignored the evidence. In fact, their ability to ignore the evidence has left us a legacy that is undeniably special. I always feel patronized when I am told that we Blacks should pride ourselves in being "descendants of African kings and queens." In a world in which Senator Barack Obama and Vice President Dick Cheney are cousins, every one of us probably has some royal blood and it's probably just as likely to be European as African. However, there is one (more) thing I know for sure. There is something transcendent, and perhaps regal, about the legacy we have inherited.

We Black people are descendants of a people who possessed a spirit that could not be suppressed. We are the descendants of a people who were subjected to the worst physical and psychological torture imaginable, from slavery to the Jim Crow South, and not only survived but thrived. We are descendants of people who would not die despite a nation's best attempt to kill them, a people that resisted the collective might of what would become the mightiest nation in the world. Our legacy is special because our ancestors ignored the evidence, evidence much more daunting than ours. Our history of surviving and thriving despite this daunting evidence should be a source of universal pride and inspiration among Black people. However, we Black people do not always choose to see it that way.

It is no accident that so many successful people regardless of race have had their successes forged through adversity. A diamond is created when a rock endures extreme pressure. With the "extreme pressure" we have endured throughout our history, one could argue that we as African Americans have a diamond-encrusted future awaiting us should we position ourselves to claim it. Knowing our history, why would we ever doubt ourselves? Our history should be the proof that we can excel in any circumstance and despite any obstacle if we are sufficiently motivated. Our history should cause us to believe that we can stage a movement that would change the world. Oh, wait a minute. We have already done that once before. Why not once more? Yet so many of us see this history, our history, as the cause of the disadvantages that exist for us today rather than a reminder of the significantly larger disadvantages we have overcome. What would happen if we all loved our legacy? What would happen if we all saw our legacy as a gift rather than a curse?

Many of us do. Without question, many Blacks today are wildly successful, and some are among the most successful people our world has ever known. But in light of all the disadvantages that come with living Black in America, how can we possibly explain such success? Did these wildly successful Blacks just get lucky like blind squirrels that find nuts? Are they simply so talented that they could not have been held down by any society, no matter how biased? Were they just the chosen ones "allowed" to be successful by a nefarious power structure in order to keep the rest of us just hopeful enough to stay in line? I believe the answer is "None of the above."

I believe these wildly successful Blacks view being Black in a different way, a special way, which allows them to excel despite being fully aware of the evidence. These successful Black people have discovered the balance between being "color-blind," dangerously unaware of the perils they face due to their race, and "color-blinded," so hyper-aware of the perils that this awareness prevents all achievement. A Black person who is color-blind may be at risk, but one who is "color-blinded" is in much greater danger. I believe these successful Blacks have found the cure for "color-blindedness." We must all find the cure for color-blindedness before it is too late.

Ignore the Evidence?

But how can we ignore all that evidence? The evidence confronts us wherever we turn. For example, according to some scholars, the financial disparity between Blacks and whites, or the "cost of being Black" is so high that it cannot possibly be overcome without dramatic government intervention. Harvard University professor of social ethics Mahzarin Banaji and Ohio State psychology professors Philip Mazzocco and Timothy Brock performed a study that estimated "the cost of being Black." The professors calculated this "cost" by estimating the wealth accumulated by whites from slavery through the Jim Crow era and wealth accumulation denied Blacks by discriminatory laws and practices during the same time period. According to this study, the "cost of being Black" could only be overcome by significant reparations in the form of a transfer of wealth from white households to Black households of a minimum of $150,000 per Black household. The professors argue that "making reparations possible is the most authentic path to realizing the dream" articulated by Dr. King forty-five years ago. Given the unlikelihood that such a transfer of wealth would ever occur, these professors in effect argue that the Black community is living deep in an economic hole from which we will never emerge.

This is our history, but what about our prospects for the future? Not surprisingly, there is ample evidence to suggest that being Black, even in 2008, means having a harder, less successful life than the average white American. The National Urban League (NUL), the prestigious nearly one hundred-year-old organization created to "enable African Americans to secure economic self-reliance, parity, power and civil rights," released its annual report describing the Black condition entitled *2008 The State of Black America.* In this report, the NUL describes dimensions upon which it measures and evaluates the quality of the Black condition. The aggregate measure of these dimensions is called the National Urban League Equality Index (NULEI). The NULEI measures the "relative status" between Blacks and whites in America. In *2008 The State of Black America,* the NULEI measured 73 percent or, said differently, Blacks are 73 percent "as equal" as whites. The key dimensions of the index and the relative scores are as follows: economics (56 percent), education (78 percent), health (76 percent), social justice (72 percent) and civic engagement (104 percent). The NUL evidence suggests that were it not for Blacks' disproportionately high engagement in civic matters, our equality as defined here would be even worse.

The evidence does not paint a pretty picture. But we don't need any evidence to convince us that a Black life can be a hard life. The great work done by the National Urban League and the aforementioned professors notwithstanding, we do not need Exhibits A through Z as proof of the condition of the Black community. Sometimes, the evidence of our condition is all we can see. We don't need a study to confirm that Blacks are over-represented in prisons and under-represented in colleges. We don't need the aid of statistics to know that as many needles are found in haystacks as Blacks found in the executive board rooms of *Fortune* 500 companies.

But we also don't need the data to know we have to accept our share of the blame for our current condition. We don't need the six o'clock news to tell us that unconscionably too often when a Black person finds himself or herself staring down the barrel of a gun, there is another Black person holding that gun. We can't avoid the evidence that too many of our children are born disadvantaged due to poor choices that we ourselves have made. We are well aware of our condition. A patient admitted to a hospital in our condition would be rushed to the ICU. Ignoring this evidence is neither simple nor prudent.

These are the facts in evidence as we know them. However, the verdict to be rendered from this evidence is still very much an open question. Some will view this evidence and conclude that we Blacks are predisposed to lower levels of academic achievement and, therefore, professional achievement. They will see this evidence as proof that Blacks in general are lacking the discipline or the moral rectitude required to be successful. We have seen this verdict rendered against us time and time again. Outside opinion notwithstanding, this is not the verdict that most concerns me.

Regrettably, more and more often, we Blacks seem to be rendering this same negative verdict on ourselves. Too often, Black people see this evidence as proof that "the system" is inexorably rigged against us and conclude that a rigged game is not worth playing. Too many of us are checking out. Too often, we take the evidence as proof that we are better off aiming low and therefore protecting ourselves from the disappointment of failing to reach loftier goals. Too often, we fail to hold each other accountable for pursuing excellence. We understand our challenges all too well and therefore we alibi our failures far too quickly. Collectively, we lower our standard of excellence until our standard no longer represents excellence at all.

We have always had an "evidence" problem, but never a more dangerous one than we do today. We have always struggled to be judged fairly, but never have we struggled so mightily against ourselves. This evidence threatens to leave us "color-blinded," so preoccupied with the challenges presented by our race that we are unable to see the height of our potential. The disease of color-blindedness is one to which we cannot afford to succumb. The aim of this book is to make sure as many Blacks as possible get the antidote.

"I Just Can't Help It"

"I love Black people. I just can't help it." I heard Tavis Smiley say this on the radio once and it really stuck with me. This phrase so accurately captures how so many of us feel, doesn't it? Don't most of us have a "rooting interest" when it comes to Black folk? It's the reason so many of us started watching golf when Tiger Woods "took it over" in the mid-1990s. It's the reason Usher outsells Justin Timberlake in the 'hood. We can relate to Usher because we "know" Usher even if we don't know him personally. The triumphs and the struggles, the joys and the pains of Black people are familiar to us because we have lived them ourselves. Sometimes the Black people we know only from afar seem just like family to us, and love of family is not something that needs to be taught. Love of family happens naturally. It's natural for Black people to root for other Black people.

Historically, the fact that Black people rooted for one another was not just a "love thing" but a practical matter as well. During times when the door of opportunity was triple-padlocked shut for all of us, any visible glimmer of daylight brought with it the hope that we would all someday see the sun. So we rooted for Black people to see daylight. Jackie Robinson's success with the Brooklyn Dodgers touched us all although most of us were not on the Dodgers' payroll. The seismic victory of the Montgomery Bus Boycott sent aftershocks of hope throughout the entire Black community and emboldened us to believe that similar tremors could be created throughout the nation. The myriad of Black celebrities who used their celebrity to advance our social causes in years past are the shoulders upon which we stand today as we attempt to rock the mic on our own personal stages. Not too long ago, we all felt without equivocation that our brother's win or our sister's win was our own personal win too. Rooting for each other, helping each other, loving each other was simply rooting for, helping, and loving ourselves. But how well do we love ourselves or each other today?

"I love Black people. I just can't help it." But I can't help but think we have a "love problem." The love we have for ourselves and for each other have changed to our detriment. Nearly two generations ago, we forced the mightiest nation in the world to begin to grant us the full citizenship it promised some one hundred years earlier. Back then, we loved our collective interests more than our individual ones. Back then, we loved our collective freedom more than we feared the individual price we had to pay to secure it. Had that price not been paid, there is no telling how we would be living today. We also seemed to love ourselves more back then too. Back then, we Black people loved ourselves enough to die, literally and figuratively, for opportunity. We prided ourselves on making a way from no way, on making "a dollar outta fifteen cents." Today, we don't seem to love ourselves enough to seize and maximize the opportunities available to us. Our "love problem" has us in deep trouble.

Simply put, Black people are a people in peril. There can be no denying that we are struggling simply to survive. Even as the most successful Blacks are enjoying unprecedented success, the Black community as a whole is drowning, struggling to keep its head above the water's surface. No matter the measure, be it wealth growth rates, graduation rates, incarceration rates, health rates, or crime rates, we are a far less successful people than we should be. We are struggling to demonstrate the same love for ourselves and for each other that propelled us to such remarkable accomplishments nearly two generations ago. We are struggling to live up to our storied, or dare I say regal, legacy. However, we can. Yes, we can! Not only can we live up to the legacy we inherited, but we can dramatically improve the legacy our next generation will enjoy. But there is one thing we must start doing today.

Believing in Love

We must believe in love. Ironically, even as we struggle to see our success potential through the blizzard of evidence to the contrary, there is one aspect of our lives in which we successfully ignore the evidence every day. Every day, we suspend disbelief to place our faith in something for which we have no good explanation. How so? We all believe in love.

The more experience we gain in life, the more we realize how little we know about love. We don't know how to reliably find love or how to reliably keep it. We can't even define love. The one thing we do know about love is that it hurts. We know that no one can hurt you like loved ones because to them we are the most vulnerable. Love doesn't often work out and, even when it does for a while, there is still better than an even chance that it will end with *"everything you own is in a box to the left."* Yet we still believe in love and desperately want it in our lives. Not one of us would want to live life without love. We will endure untold horrors for love's sake. Why? We don't know. It just is. When it comes to love, we know to ignore the evidence. We know that having love is worth the struggle. Isn't our success as individuals and as a people worth the struggle too? Why can't we believe in our success, individually and as a Black community, with the same tenacity as we believe in love?

We can and we must believe in love. We must love ourselves and each other enough to do the work of success. With this book, I will argue with all my might that we, the Black community, must accept on faith that we will succeed. This faith, this love, will be the foundation upon which our renaissance as a Black community must be built. We must accept our destiny of success in the same way we accept that we deserve to be loved. If we do not, we will not survive. We must believe in love, but what does this really mean in the context of race and success?

We Black people must love ourselves enough as individuals to get out of our own way. No excuse is acceptable, least of all our race, to justify anything less than the all-out pursuit of excellence. The wildly successful Blacks who live among us and those who lived before us have proven the strength of our own will is infinite when applied properly. Does this mean that the weight of racism exists only in our own minds? No. However, the most successful Blacks believe they, and only they, decide how they should carry its weight or if they should carry it at all. They do not concede one inch of success to racism.

These successful Blacks often live in direct contradiction to the life philosophies and coping strategies regarding race many of us accept as given. Often, they have abandoned the commonly held beliefs that have guided us in the Black community for so long but that today work to our detriment. Inside the minds of these successful Blacks resides the best and boldest thinking, the most audaciously hopeful thinking, on race and success. Throughout this book, I will share this audaciously hopeful thinking with you directly from its source, a cross-section of successful Black people just like you. Yes, just like you. The fact that you are reading this book means you have success and love on your mind. This is where all success begins, grows, and is sustained in one's mind and heart. We can all learn how to create a reality for ourselves in which the negative impact of racism is not a given, even when the presence of racism is given. We will learn.

We must love our Black community enough to put each other first in our thoughts and actions. Too often, out of misguided self-interest, we aim our attacks at the wrong enemy, ourselves. We have to keep the well-being of our community top of mind in all of our thoughts and actions. We must find a way to turn our every day frustrations into the motivation to take positive action. We must learn that burning down our own house, literally or figuratively, is an abysmal means of protest serving only those who oppose us.

We have to channel our rage in ways that makes us better. The peer pressure we apply on each other needs to motivate success, not failure. If we do nothing else, we must break our self-destructive tendency to search for ways to strip Blacks of their "membership cards" by claiming they are not "real" enough for us. If we can't help each other, then we need to, at the very least, get out of the way. But we must conclude that "out of the way" is not good enough. We must find a way to embrace the collective pursuit of success. Together, we can develop new rules of engaging each other that serve to uplift us rather than to undermine us. We can learn to demonstrate our love for each other more often and to greater positive effect. We will learn.

We must love our children enough to refuse to leave them our unfinished business. Five generations ago, we fought for, died for, and won our physical emancipation. In the generations that followed, we have battled tooth and nail for legal emancipation, full and fair access to the political, legal, and economic systems. While this battle is not over, we have gained a tremendous amount of opposition territory. Every generation since the end of slavery has left a better situation for its children than the one it inherited. They all handled their business. Will we handle ours?

It is our obligation to advance the causes important to Black people such that our children can stand on our shoulders and reach significantly higher ground. We cannot allow our children to be consumed, as we so often are, by the fool's errand of debating why person "x" used racial slur "y." Instead we must focus upon teaching our children how "x" and "y" complete algebraic equations. We cannot afford to leave our children to fight battles we should have already won or, worse still, to regain ground we have lost. We must learn how to focus upon and fight the real battles rather than taking the (race) bait of engaging in meaningless, ancillary, and ultimately counterproductive ones. We will learn.

So what are the "real battles?" We must start to conquer the final frontier in our battle for equality. This final frontier is not enacting a new law or terminating a long standing discriminatory practice. The final frontier is changing our own attitudes toward race and success. The final battle is to free our minds so the next generation may live free. Dr. Martin Luther King, Jr., as was so often the case, captured this notion so eloquently when he said:

> *As long as the mind is enslaved, the body can never be free. No Lincoln Emancipation Proclamation, no Johnsonian civil rights bill can totally bring this kind of freedom. The Negro will only be free when he reaches down to the inner depths of his own being and signs…his own emancipation proclamation.*

We will only be free of the burden racism places on our pursuit of success when we begin to think differently about race and success. This is a not a problem we can look to anyone else to solve.

Thankfully, this is not a problem that we need outside help to solve. We can and we must think differently on our own. We must answer our own questions. How do we get out of our own way? How should we put each other first? How can we lighten the mental load racism places upon us so our children will not have to carry the same weight? As we will see throughout this book, the blueprint is already in place. Some of us are already living it. The answers to our questions are hiding in plain sight. The answers start and end with love. Therefore, this is my *Love Letter to Black People.*

CHAPTER ONE
THE OBAMA EPIPHANY

I began writing *Love Letter* on July 27, 2004. This was not the date I started to put pen to paper, but the date I began to receive the inspiration that would become *Love Letter.* July 27, 2004 was the day Senator Barack Obama vaulted onto the international stage at the 2004 Democratic National Convention and, as we know now, began to change the course of American history. The positive reaction to the speech he delivered that evening, entitled "The Audacity of Hope," propelled him from "out of nowhere" as a state senator from Illinois to U.S. senator and the author of two best-selling books to the Democratic Party's 2008 presidential nominee to the favorite to become the forty-fourth president of the United States in less than four years. Of course, none of us knew any of that was coming. However, many of us knew we were watching something special that night.

"Special" is a gross understatement of how I now view that evening. From the moment Obama started to speak, I sat straight up in my bed and was transfixed by his message. By the time he was finished, I had tears in my eyes. For the first time in my life, I truly believed an African American could be elected president of the United States in my lifetime. That night I said the words aloud, "I have just seen the first Black president of the United States," to assure myself I had not dreamt what I had just seen. Perhaps I said those words to try to speak that crazy dream—and even then it was crazy—into existence. That night, I bought into Obama's "audacity of hope" message wholeheartedly, a message that would become the title of his second book and the theme of his presidential campaign. But more importantly, that night an inspired thought began to grow in my mind and I started to think differently about race and success.

There's Something About Barack

Clearly, I am not the only one who sees something special in Barack Obama. No group of people is more excited about Obama than African Americans. We gave him our near-unanimous support in the Democratic primaries despite the fact he was running against a member of the "First Family" of the Democratic Party, Senator Hillary Clinton, and the spouse of the so-called "First Black President," former President Bill Clinton. Perhaps if we knew we would have an actual African American to support in the race for the presidency so soon, we would not have been so willing to give President Clinton the "Black President" moniker so easily. Not only did we support Obama in record numbers during the Democratic primaries, but we threatened to excommunicate any African American who had the audacity (there's that word again) to support anyone else. Congresspersons Maxine Waters, John Lewis, and Charles Rangel, to name a few, caught untold grief for backing Senator Clinton during the Democratic Party primaries. So many African Americans were and still are decidedly displeased that these African American leaders chose to stand between Barack Obama and history. They could taste the possibility of an African American president and were in no mood to have the dream thwarted by one of our own. I attended several African American events during the primary season at which the mere mention of the name "Barack Obama" inspired an ovation. He went from an unknown to Black royalty in a hot minute. There is no doubt that we Blacks have much love for Obama.

However, Obama does not just have "race appeal." Anyone who understands math knows that no one can be a serious presidential candidate with simply "race appeal." There have been other Black U.S. presidential candidates and they all have received strong support from the Black community. However, you can't win elections in Iowa, Colorado, or Wisconsin as did Obama on "race appeal" alone. Barack Obama has much more than simply "race appeal." To this point in the election cycle, Barack has accomplished something for which we have no precedent. There's something about Barack, something fundamentally different about the campaign he leads.

In fact, the Obama campaign is less like a political campaign and more like a movement. Obama is drawing concert-sized crowds to political rallies. He has grown folks screaming like teenagers at a Michael Jackson concert circa *Thriller.* Of course, it's not unusual for African Americans to have high Q ratings among non-Blacks. However, those widely admired African Americans generally rap, sing, make people laugh, or do something with a ball. None of them have been allowed anywhere near the "red phone" or the "button." But people don't just like this brother. They are backing him hard! The Obama campaign has contribution dollars leaping out of more pockets and in larger piles than anyone in the history of American politics. More significantly, people of all races are entrusting him with their hopes, their dreams, and their futures. He has made political activists out of people who were steadfastly apathetic until now. He has made political engagement cool again. And a Black man inspired this? What planet are we on?

Maybe mainstream society doesn't know Obama is Black. Not hardly. In fact, there has never been a successful politician with a name more ill-suited to American political success than Barack Hussein Obama. His last name is uncomfortably close to the first name of the man in the pole position on America's Most Wanted list, Osama bin Laden. He also shares a name with Saddam Hussein, the Iraqi dictator that burrowed so far under the Bush family's skin that the United States re-wrote its foreign policy playbook (creating the so-called "Bush Doctrine" which condones preventative war) to justify taking him out. The only way Obama could have a worse name for politics in America is if his parents had named him "Adolf" rather than Barack. There is no doubt that he would smell sweeter to the general public if the rose that is Obama went by any other name.

So what makes Obama so appealing, so successful? What makes so many people of all races claim Obama as one of their own? What makes so many people so comfortable with the idea of a Black man named "Obama" occupying the Oval Office when the notion was so incredibly foreign until now? And most importantly, what lessons can we Blacks learn from his success to bring about success in our own lives?

The Post-Racial Messenger

Since Dr. King delivered his legendary "I Have a Dream" speech, countless people have urged and advocated, spoken and written about the desirability of a post-racial world, one in which people are "judged not by the color of their skin, but by the content of their character." Most would agree there is an upside for everyone in such a post-racial world. Our national obsession with race, although it spreads its burden unequally, is a burden to all Americans. People of color have to account for racism on a daily basis, navigating around, over, and through an obstacle course that many whites do not appreciate, will not acknowledge exists, or become resentful at its mere mention. Whites are burdened by race as well, often being "presumed racist" and held accountable for thoughts they don't have or actions for which they were not responsible. Undoubtedly, the vast majority of Americans regardless of race would prefer to live in Dr. King's dream than in present day America. Yet, in our heart of hearts, most of us viewed Dr. King's dream as an impossible dream, an aspirational world with no hope of becoming reality. Then Barack Obama arrived.

Simply put, Barack Obama has made millions, regardless of race, believe in an impossible dream. Obama has caused Americans everywhere to rethink and even change their definitions of "us." His appeal is rooted in his ability to credibly articulate a vision of a "post-racial world" to a large, diverse audience. His post-racial message resonates with millions of whites because Obama refuses to be the representative of African American grievances. Of course, this approach flies completely in the face of the approach favored by many of our most prominent Black leaders today. Yet Obama gives no indication that he holds the problems of African Americans in higher regard than those of other Americans.

Instead, Obama describes Black problems the same way he describes Hispanic, Asian-American, or white problems. They are all American problems that all Americans have an equal vested interest in solving. Obama seeks to be an American leader; that is, a leader to all Americans. Thus he has no interest in leading in a fashion that appeals to only a fraction of the American population, even if the fractional group is the one to which he most closely identifies, African Americans. As a result, there are now millions of Americans who believe a post-racial world is not a place we must wait for or hope to inhabit, but a place we can and will create. Millions believe that, as Obama often says, *"We are the change that we seek."* Of course, for this change to actually take place, millions of those millions of believers must be African Americans.

But why do so many people of all races believe that Barack Obama can lead America into its post-racial era? What makes him different than the legions of other Black leaders before him who have echoed Dr. King's "content of their character" refrain? He is different because he thinks differently about race and reacts differently to "racial situations" than most of his predecessors. Perhaps Obama's one-of-a-kind background makes him uniquely unencumbered by the "conventional Black wisdom" regarding race.

The man who would be the first African American U.S. president, in fact, has no African American parents. His late mother was a white Kansan and his late father was an African exchange student from Kenya. He was raised during the bulk of his childhood in Hawaii and Indonesia, both places in which he was even more of an outsider than is the average African American in America. When Obama returned to the "mainland," he earned a place at two of the finest universities in America, Columbia University and Harvard University, where again he was gazing upon the mainstream from the outside in. Upon graduation from Harvard Law School as the first African American president of the *Harvard Law Review* and with his ticket to mainstream success punched, he made an interesting decision.

After living his entire life up to this point as an outsider, Obama chose to "opt-in" to African American culture fully, embracing it in a way that others with his background may not have. Obama did not just dip his toe into African American culture but completely immersed himself in it personally by marrying an African American woman and professionally by beginning his life's work as a civil rights attorney in inner-city Chicago. Despite finding his cultural home within the Black community, Obama was unquestionably influenced by his life as the perpetual outsider. Undoubtedly, Obama's diverse set of experiences has provided him the insight he uses to chart a different course for his success in the context of race.

It is likely this perpetual outsider status served as the foundation for the life philosophy and, later, the political message that would bring Obama so much success. Maybe never fitting cleanly in any racial environment causes him to broaden his definition of "we." Maybe this caused him to truly understand there are many more ways in which "we" are united than divided. His unique set of experiences in terms of race gives him a moral credibility that few enjoy from which to articulate the complexity of the race issue. This singular set of life experiences has also helped him avoid the race traps that have befallen so many would-be successful Blacks who came before him. Obama clearly "gets it," but what is the "it?"

Refusing the Bait

Does mainstream society know Barack Obama is Black? Of course it does. As if his image on TV screens was not enough proof of his racial identity, Obama's political opponents have been shouting it from the rooftops to make sure no one misses the point. Why? Because the discussion of race is the "third rail" in politics, a topic so highly charged it is fatal to the touch. The race discussion, in some ways, is an equal opportunity force, "electrocuting" public figures of all ethnicities for failing to respect its power. White politicians get zapped by the race discussion by making statements which are seen as racially insensitive. Black politicians fall victim to the race discussion by making statements seen as reverse racist or by reacting too angrily to perceived racist statements, thereby feeding negative stereotypes about Black people scaring the mainstream in the process.

In today's politics, often one good zap is good enough to end a political career. Obama has steadfastly tried not to be the "race candidate," yet he has been doing most of the talking regarding race. Why? Obama's political opponents are trying to get him to take the bait, the race bait. They hope the more he speaks about race, the more likely he is to get that one good zap. They hope Obama will give them that one angry tirade, after which the mainstream media will dance him off the stage like Sandman on Showtime at the Apollo. Obama understands the power of the third rail and the impact it would have on his ability to successfully complete his mission. This is the "it" Obama gets. Obama knows the stakes, so he refuses the bait. He always refuses to take the bait.

In fact, Obama has been leading the American political discourse on race without becoming a victim of the discussion. How? He has deftly avoided taking the race bait when it is offered, no matter who does the offering. The race bait often looks "tasty," but taking the bait always serves to increase fear or anger between races or discord and divisiveness within races. The race bait serves to kill success for those who take it like a hook often kills the fish that bites it. Obama understands that his political opponents are trying to (race) bait him into appearing frightening to a mainstream society that has been conditioned to fear Black males. Obama has stubbornly avoided the "Angry Black Man" moment that would play directly to those fears and possibly doom his campaign. Further, Obama has avoided the costly racially insensitive gaffe (a la Reverend Jesse Jackson's "Hymie-town" debacle) that would invalidate his moral standing to lead America into a post-racial era. Obama refuses to fall into the old patterns regarding race that have been the undoing of so many would-be successful Blacks.

If you look closely, we have seen this approach before from our African American standard bearers. Obama's approach to the issue of race is very reminiscent of that of Jackie Robinson and, dare I say, Dr. King. The most successful of our standard bearers knew intuitively that they would be held to a higher moral standard than their adversaries and, therefore, could not play the game as they did. They had to place the success of the mission ahead of their human instinct to attack when attacked. Jackie Robinson, as the first Black Major League baseball player in the modern era, could not respond to the overly aggressive behavior of his opponents in kind. He knew that an equally aggressive reply, even if justified, would be seen as proof that he, and by extension all Blacks, were not fit to be Major League baseball players.

Similar to Robinson, Dr. King chose to lead non-violent protests in the face of the extreme violence directed toward him and his fellow protestors. Of course, as a practical matter, violent protests were not a viable option as Dr. King and his protestors could not have armed themselves sufficiently to face down the U.S. government. However, Dr. King was also aware that any violence on the part of the protestors, even in self-defense, would have been seen as justification for more violence against them. He, too, understood that, as the standard bearer, he would be held to a higher moral standard. As Robinson and King before him, Obama has remained disciplined, living at a higher standard than his political opponents because he knows the responsibility and the burden of the standard barrier. He understands it takes more discipline and more mental toughness to walk away from a self-destructive battle than it does to stay and fight. It is harder to refuse the bait than to take it.

Ironically, it was Obama's alleged lack of toughness that was at the center of Senator Clinton's case for her candidacy for president. This was the race bait for which she wanted Obama to reach, the hook she hoped he would bite. Senator Hillary Clinton consistently claimed to be the "toughest"

Democratic candidate in the race, and by inference that Obama lacked toughness. Often this "toughness" was defined by the veracity with which she attacked her political opponents, including Obama. Obama's decision to refuse to build his "toughness quotient" with attacks in kind caused ABC News online to write an article about him entitled "The Sissyness of Hope?" Being called, in effect, a "sissy" by a white woman repeatedly and publically would cause many a Black man to come completely unhinged. However, had Obama reacted angrily to this line of attack, he would have confirmed negative racial stereotypes many Americans have of Black men and surely damaged his chances to become the president. Instead, Obama maintained his cool.

Refusing the bait is difficult in general and probably especially difficult for Obama in this case. Had Obama been a politician without the additional responsibility of being a standard bearer, he may have considered Senator Clinton an easy target for conventional political attacks. From her many years in public life and the many scandals with which she was allegedly associated, Obama could have leveled any number of attacks at her to score political points. As satisfying as it may have felt to strike back, he knew there was a hook under that tasty worm. His political attacks would not have been as the normal political tit-for-tat. They would have been seen as a demonstration that he, and all Black people, was unfit to lead. Obama knew better, simply too wise to take the bait. In the process, Obama has showed a different type of toughness, a mental toughness demonstrated by trailblazers like Dr. King and Jackie Robinson. A standard bearer must put the mission ahead of his or her ego and anger.

Barack has not allowed himself to be goaded into taking the race bait when offered by Blacks either. In fact, his dramatic departure from the approach of civil rights era Black leaders earned Obama criticism and derision from Black community leaders Jesse Jackson and former United Nations Ambassador Andrew Young early in his campaign. Jesse Jackson accused Obama of "acting white" for the measured tone Obama took when responding to the "Jena 6" controversy. Andrew Young mocked Obama by suggesting former President Bill Clinton was "more Black" than is Obama, even going so far as to cite President Clinton's sexual habits as proof. Huh? Again, Obama was too wise to fall for the trap. By trying to prove his "Blackness" to the old guard, he would have jeopardized his chance to realize the dream for which the old guard claims to be fighting. It takes toughness to endure being called "unworthy" by the legends of your community, even the fading ones, without slipping into the self-sabotage of engaging in backward-looking racial rhetoric. Obama won't even allow the Black community to goad him into an act of self-sabotage.

Obama understands that reacting the way Blacks typically do when faced with issues of race is a losing strategy. He understands that allowing himself to be angered by taunts from the majority is an invitation to self-sabotage. Historically, this has been a reliable way to thin the ranks of Black contenders for power, influence, and success. We have been so quick to anger and overreact when taunted that we can be counted upon by our opposition to destroy our own chances for success. Further, Obama understands that responding to the charges of treason from his own people is only a distraction averting his gaze from the real prize. Too often, we Black people injure ourselves in meaningless intramural scrimmages that cause us to lose the most important games. Obama is successful because he is beyond retrospective thinking on race and therefore knows better than to fall for the race bait no matter who offers it. A standard bearer must always know better. Note to Black people: We are all standard barriers.

The strength of Obama's focus on the prize despite the many attempts to distract him leaves one fact abundantly clear. He is completely unencumbered by the self-destructive mental race traps that doom so many of us Blacks. He is not crippled by the expectation of racism. He does not live his life convinced of the existence of "The Man," the nefarious anti-Black bogeyman waiting behind the curtain to thwart all significant Black success at the most psychologically damaging moment. He is not part of the "Keeping It Real" police, the Black people among us who expect uniform thinking on all issues that impact the Black community and stand ready to excommunicate "wrong thinkers" with the slurs "sellout" or "race traitor." He does not feel compelled by his empathy of our collective plight to excuse our own bad behavior and therefore damn us to perpetually repeat the same bad behavior. Said differently, he is not carrying the same mental weight due to his race that so many of us do.

This is not to say the weight of racism is all in our minds. However, we Black people regularly add to the weight we must bear with additional tonnage we do not have to bear. It is Obama's freedom from the self-imposed portion of the weight of racism that has driven Obama's rise to prominence or, perhaps more correctly, pre-eminence. By studying this freedom of mind, we can start to understand the blueprint for how we as a people can replicate this success.

Without this weight, the encumbrance that many Blacks feel when it comes to race, Obama has been able to move to the precipice of the Holy Grail of Black achievement. He is poised to do the one thing "The Man" was sworn never to allow. He has arrived at this precipice with an approach unlike any Black leader before him. He has more than just a "puncher's chance" of becoming the president. In fact, some people would call him the favorite at this point. I am sure this statement alone scares the mess out of those who jockey for the fictional title of "President of Black America." If the president of the United States of America were Black, the folly of the messages and approaches of the would-be presidents of Black America would become even more obvious. Perhaps this groundbreaking event in the history of our nation would make us all realize it is time to think differently about race and success. Barack Obama, the favorite to be elected the president of the United States of America? This statement alone should also give Black people a tremendous amount of hope for the future. This statement alone should make us all sit straight up in our beds.

What is the lesson here for Black people? What should we be learning from the success of Barack Obama? Barack Obama is successful because he has moved past the retrospective thinking regarding the race and failed responses to it. He knows that Blacks are expected to lose control when taunted racially, but he refuses to live down to those expectations. The taunts of which we must be leery are not simply insults hurled directly at us as individuals, but also racially charged situations created to invoke our historically self-destructive reactions. When we react as expected to the taunt, we dance on another man's string at his behest and for his pleasure. We are being played. Obama doesn't allow himself to be played. Regarding race, he is no one's Pinocchio, so he will not allow anyone to play the Geppetto role in his life. We cannot allow our strings to be pulled by issues of race.

"There's something going on here"

"There's something going on here." This is a line from Obama's stump speech in which he describes a movement that started for him on the old Capitol building steps in Springfield, Illinois, and promises to continue in a new home at 1600 Pennsylvania Avenue. However, there is something else going on here. Obama has illuminated the blueprint for how we Black people must view our pursuit of success in the context of race. I say "illuminated" rather than "created" because so many Black people like you, as we will see throughout *Love Letter,* are already living at least part of the blueprint and enjoying tremendous success as a result. Through his campaign, Obama has illuminated the possibilities available to us when we refuse to take the race bait by employing the same losing strategies regarding issues of race.

Throughout his campaign, he has not turned a blind eye to race, but he has refused to become blinded by race either. In fact, at the height of the "Jeremiah Wright controversy," Obama gave a speech about race that was perhaps the most honest, intelligent, thoughtful speech on the topic we have ever heard an elected official give. MSNBC's Chris Matthews called the speech the "best speech ever given on race in this country" and even Major Garrett of Fox News, a network usually not friendly to Democrats, called it "uniquely honest."

Through his actions, Obama is telling us and showing us that the 1960s' view of the race struggle that so many of us possess no longer serves us. It fact, it damages us in so many ways. If we pay close attention to the

Obama phenomenon, beyond the crowds, beyond the hype, beyond the racially motivated pride, we will see a new way to view race and success. We will each find the will to refuse the race bait. *"There's something going on here."*

The blueprint for the mindset that will drive our future success as a Black community was no more in evidence than during that seminal speech at the 2004 Democratic National Convention, the "Audacity of Hope" speech. Perhaps Obama's greatest gift is his ability to speak directly into the hearts and minds of so many people of different backgrounds. The genius of the "Audacity of Hope" message that evening was that it spoke directly to us, to the African American condition, but not only the African American condition. Obama's target audience, of course, was much wider. He was speaking to a national audience to make the case for a John Kerry-John Edwards administration that would never come to pass. Nevertheless, his message was at once specific to us and universal. He was speaking to all Americans, but I could not help but notice how relevant his message was to our African American condition. It was through the themes of this speech that I started to see how we must view race differently.

Obama said: *It's not enough for just some of us to prosper—for alongside our famous individualism, there's another ingredient in the American saga, a belief that we're all connected as one people. It is that fundamental belief—It is that fundamental belief: I am my brother's keeper. I am my sister's keeper that makes this country work. It's what allows us to pursue our individual dreams and yet still come together as one American family.*

I heard: It is imperative that we in the Black community rediscover the notion that we as individuals are not in competition with each other in our pursuit of success. We are engaged in one struggle, not thirty-eight million struggles. Not one of us, no matter how successful, can live completely unaffected by the plight of the Black community. We are inexorably tied to each other, buoyed by our collective successes and weighted down by our collective failures. We have a true vested interest in each other. Our ability to rediscover that connection will determine our future success.

Obama said: *Now even as we speak, there are those who are preparing to divide us—the spin masters, the negative ad peddlers who embrace the politics of "anything goes." Well, I say to them tonight, there is not a liberal America and a conservative America—there is the United States of America. There is not a Black America and a White America and Latino America and Asian America—there's the United States of America.*

I heard: We the Black community are not served by the incessant pursuit to figure out who is "really Black" and who is a "sellout." Every minute we spend trying to "out" someone and expel them from the Black community is a minute we don't spend solving a real problem. We don't have to accept the short-sighted, small-minded notion that there are only so many spots available for successful Blacks. There is not a finite amount of allowable Black success over which we must fight. We don't have to behave like crabs in a barrel. We can destroy the barrel. We must find a way to destroy the "crabs in a barrel" mindset and replace it with one that encourages us to collaborate. We must figure out how to resist the urge to divide ourselves, as such division makes us more susceptible to being conquered.

Obama said: *I'm not talking about blind optimism here—the almost willful ignorance that thinks unemployment will go away if we just don't think about it, or the health care crisis will solve itself if we just ignore it. That's not what I'm talking about. I'm talking about something more substantial. It's the hope of slaves sitting around a fire singing freedom songs; the hope of immigrants setting out for distant shore…the hope of a skinny kid with a funny name who believes that America has a place for him too. Hope—Hope in the face of difficulty. Hope in the face of uncertainty. The audacity of hope!*

I heard: We, the Black community, have to ignore the evidence. We face no current obstacle greater than the ones we have already overcome. The only obstacle that can impede us is the belief that our success is impossible. The only opponent that can defeat us is the belief that we are not supposed to be united. The only force that can destroy us is us.

Obama said: *I believe that we have a righteous wind at our backs and that as we stand on the crossroads of history, we can make the right choices and meet the challenges that face us.*

I heard: Greatness as a people is ours if we choose it. We must love our greatness more than we fear its price. We can choose to change our minds about race and therefore start to change the world. We must do it now. Today is the day we must choose to be color-blinded no more. A post-racial, "content of (our) character" world is one in which we deserve to live. However, we must make it so.

Obama said: A*merica! Tonight, if you feel the same energy that I do, if you feel the same urgency that I do, if you feel the same passion that I do, if you feel the same hopefulness that I do—if we do what we must do, then I have no doubt that all across the country, from Florida to Oregon, from Washington to Maine, the people will rise up—and this country will reclaim its promise, and out of this long political darkness a brighter day will come."*

I heard: We must feel the urgency of now. We must understand that we too can awaken and emerge from our long darkness. We too can reclaim our promise. We do not have one more moment to waste.

Just Words?

Barack Obama's political opponents have tried to use his skill as an orator against him. They suggest because he is an exceptional speaker, by definition, he is deficient in other critical areas of leadership. They shower him with faint praise, extolling his "soaring rhetoric" in order to undermine his candidacy. They say Barack's message is "just words" and words are unimportant. However, Obama's political opponents did not count on us. They failed to realize that the power of words is not in the speaker, but in the hearts of those who receive the words.

Words have power. Words have the power to harm or to heal. Words can ignite a fire that cleanses and purifies or a fire that destroys everything in its path. Words can change everything. Words can start a revolution. The power of a revolution lies in not the will of one individual, but the inspired actions of millions of individuals working in concert and feeling as if their cause is too righteous be denied. My hope is that Obama's presence and words have started a revolution among Black people. My hope is that we Black people realize our adopting a mindset that views race and success in a more productive way is a cause too righteous to be denied. This revolution will ultimately have nothing to do with Barack Obama, any one person, or political party. However, this revolution will have everything to do with millions of Black people being a party to the renaissance of the Black community. If a revolution is like a raging fire, my hope is that Love Letter will fan the flames.

There was something about the man and the message that caused me to completely change the way I view race and success. I call it the Obama Epiphany. My Obama Epiphany is the recognition that there is an important balance to be struck between being Black and being consumed by being Black. We are Black by definition, but we are not defined by being Black. Our skin tone is not the totality of our existence.

To this end, it is our turn to start some heavy lifting. Our ancestors did the heavy lifting that allows us to live physically free and, although there is still work to be done, legally free. It is now our turn to bend our backs. It is our responsibility to lighten the load of racism on our minds. This is the weight we must lift. It is our responsibility to become mentally free so our children will live free as well. However, the only way we can lead this movement is by example. The only way our children will think differently about race and success is if we show them the way.

Further, if America is to have a post-racial era, Black people will lead us there. In a very real sense, we hold the key to this better world for all Americans. We are the most visible symbol of the distance our nation has yet to travel to enjoy a post-racial society. We will be the ones to decide whether the nation moves beyond race to a "content of (our) character" era. No other segment of the American population can decide for us how we should feel about race, our history, or the legacy our history has left us. We have to do this on our own. As Dr. King said, only we can sign our freedom into existence now.

How long will to take us to sign for our freedom? As freedom is never easy and never free, are we willing to fight for this freedom or will we just hope against hope that our children can emancipate themselves? Are we tough enough to refuse the race bait when offered, no matter who does the offering? Are we willing to do the hard work to find the cure for color-blindedness? Do we love ourselves and our children enough to give this gift?

I believe we do. However, there is one barrier that will keep us from seeing the "Obama Epiphany" and marshaling its power. There is one huge barrier keeping us from recognizing the blueprint and from it building a house of prosperity. If we do not overcome this one barrier, we will never live in the world that Dr. King and now Barack Obama have described. If we fail to overcome this one barrier, it will be a mistake from which we will never recover.

CHAPTER TWO
LIVING ANGRY

"He who angers you, controls you" – **Often repeated quote**

There's a reason why extreme rage is sometimes described as "blind rage." Rage always seems to hurt the one enraged, because rage by definition is out of control. Rage leaves the enraged to clean up the results of the indiscriminate havoc wreaked. This, of course, assumes the results of the rage can be cleaned up. For mere minutes or seconds of satisfaction, the enraged will endure days, months, years, or a lifetime of grief. Rage always leaves the enraged in a worse place, like the hospital, the prison, the morgue, or at the end of a cherished relationship. With rage, life so often imitates art. In the movie *The Godfather,* the blind rage of Sonny, the eldest son of Don Vito Corleone, caused him to leave himself exposed to his eventual assassins. By contrast, the controlled aggression of Don Vito's youngest son Michael later led the family to gangster preeminence. Blind rage makes the enraged lose his or her mind. It's hard to do right when you are out of your right mind.

The one thing that reliably sends us Black folk into a blind rage is racism. If you are like me, racism in all of its forms—from its most sneaky and subtle to the most overt Klan-style racism—is your trigger. If you are like me, this is the emotion you to have to struggle most to control. This anger makes us thankful that courts do not (usually) convict for thoughts because we all would be doing hard time upstate. If you are like me, this anger is the emotion that causes you to relinquish control of yourself to the person or thing that angers you. This anger causes you to lose sight of the big picture and self-sabotage. We all have had bouts with this type of blindness. Whose neighborhoods did we destroy after Dr. King was assassinated or in the wake of the Rodney King verdict? There's a reason it's called "blind rage." This blind rage causes "color-blindedness" in Black people. Blind rage makes us lose our right minds. Blind rage causes us to move uncontrollably backward in life, further and further way from our goals. We cannot move forward until we stop succumbing to our rage, until we stop "living angry."

Mile Markers

Stop living angry? Of course, this is much more easily said than done, because we didn't start out angry. There was a time in each of our lives at which we were blissfully ignorant of our racial identity and the significance of this identity in greater society. In many ways, experiencing racism and feeling its sting is a Black rite of passage. It is the ceremony by which we "become Black" in a figurative sense, a ceremony we remember every well. We can all recall passing the many "mile markers" of racism in our journey to our present personal understanding of what it means to be Black.

As we pass these mile markers, we also feel the emotional weight of this journey: first recognition, then shame, then disappointment, and then anger. Most of us can recall dozens of our mile markers given the slightest provocation, the events in our lives that taught us that we were subject to a different set of rules than those in the majority. Despite my best efforts, I never have much trouble remembering my mile markers.

MILE MARKER – I remember my father getting edgy when I was reading Winnie the Pooh as a young child. He disliked the character Tigger the Tiger. I remember not understanding why.

MILE MARKER – I remember being a middle school student in a suburban high school who was invited repeatedly to board the bus that carried inner city transfer students from this suburban school to their inner city homes. I remember the moment of recognition, then shame. I was an interloper, someone trespassing where he didn't belong.

MILE MARKER – I remember being cut from the varsity baseball team as a junior in high school for "dubious reasons" and the baseball coach mocking my preparations to try out again as a senior. I remember being extremely disappointed.

MILE MARKER – I remember being excited about being admitted to "that university" and having a discussion about it with an acquaintance of my parents. I remember his response, "Oh, really. What sport do you play?" Of course, "that university" only admits smart students and athletes and there was no chance of me being the former. I remember being displeased.

MILE MARKER – I remember arriving at "that university" and being immediately challenged by a dorm mate about the legitimacy of my admission. Without any knowledge of my credentials or accomplishments, he declared, "You are only here because you are Black." I remember having violent thoughts.

MILE MARKER – I remember first becoming aware that some white people feared Black people and learning this fear manifested in "extra vigilance" when I was near. I remember seeing handbags clutched more tightly in my presence and my movement watched more closely when I was near the valuables. I remember thinking, "I'm not that guy."

MILE MARKER – I remember leaving the academic world for the professional one and getting a different kind of education. I remember having a conversation over the phone with a potential customer who shared bigoted comment after bigoted comment with me because he was sure he was speaking with a white person. The coast was clear for him to spew his hatred. I was so well-spoken I couldn't possibly have been Black.

MILE MARKER – I remember having an entire conversation with a work colleague as well as another individual. This colleague could not tell me and this other individual apart because we were both of similar height and Black. In fact, I remember dozens of times where I was said to "favor" someone with whom I only shared skin tone. Don't we all look alike?

MILE MARKER -- I remember having my intelligence questioned despite my credentials. I remember having my passion at work interpreted as malevolence. Sometimes, I remember every slight…every single slight. I remember…becoming angry.

Living Angry

We have a right to be angry. And to a certain degree, I'm still angry. First, I am angry we are still having the "race conversation." Why are we still talking about this? The civil rights movement began in earnest more than fifty years ago with the Montgomery Bus Boycott. In the dozen or so years that followed, the movement caught hold and forever changed us as a nation. At the height of the civil rights movement, Dr. King articulated a Dream that is just as relevant today as it was on August 28, 1963 when he made his landmark speech. *"I have a dream that my four little children will one day live in a nation where they will not be judged by the color of their skin but by the content of their character."* Please sign me up!

Yet more than forty-five years after Dr. King first articulated this Dream, the topic of race is still as divisive and incendiary as ever. More than forty-five years later, a marginally popular radio show host can still say three words that almost no one heard live and create a two-week long media controversy. Those three words were "nappy-headed ho," of course uttered by Don Imus about the Rutgers University women's basketball team. Those three words created energy within the Black community that we seldom feel about the hundreds of other issues that affect us more profoundly. Those three words caused us to become energized in a way that most pivotal issues of the day have not.

Why? Because racism is real and it still can move us, for better or worse, like no other cause can. Fifty years after the Montgomery Bus Boycott and forty years after passing legislation outlawing most legal forms of race-based discrimination, anyone who calls himself or herself Black can still feel the sting of racism on any given day. No matter our education level, our background, our wealth, or our connections, each one of us is still just a (fill-in-the-blank) to someone. Perhaps someone powerful. Every day, Blacks of all walks of life, in every corner of the country, and on every rung of the social ladder are "living angry" due to racism.

I've lived angry with the knowledge that I had to account for racism. Why should I have to accept an additional "degree of life difficulty" merely due to my ethnicity? Isn't life itself hard enough? Why after more than 140 years after the Emancipation Proclamation have I still only traded the chains of slavery for the ankle weights of racism? Granted, these weights are not nearly as heavy, but they are still much heavier than I deserve.

I've lived angry with the knowledge that I may have to teach my children the same lesson. Why are we still dealing with this tired issue? Why do we still have to teach our children about eight-tracks in an MP3 world? At ages four and two, my children are too young to understand now, but I was resentful that I may have to teach my children about this same silly standard. I was angry that I may have to make them aware that they could not expect to "win any ties," that they would have to "work twice as hard," that, as Dr. Cornel West wrote, *Race Matters.* Your mirror may say "brown," but society will say "Black" and "Black" comes with strings attached whether you like it or not. I resented that fact that I would have to teach my son about his additional burden as a Black male. He would be seen as aggressive when he is driven and threatening when he is passionate. He would have to be taught that some people have been taught to fear him and others to hate him. He would have to be taught how to counter the fear and the hate. I was angry that children born two generations after the civil rights movement began may still need to be educated in Jim Crow, not as a historical exercise but a practical one.

I've lived angry when I thought about the opportunity, the wealth, and the achievement of which I and we have undoubtedly been robbed. There were so many things that would have been rightfully mine had the world been "right." Wealth is a major, maybe the major, determining factor in so many other success factors in our society today. Pick any dimension. The more wealth you have, the more of the "good stuff" (access to education, access to health care, access to the political process, access to the legal system, access to economic opportunity…shall I go on?) you will get. African Americans were legally and systematically denied wealth for most of our nation's existence while we helped to build the wealth enjoyed by the majority. If you are an African American and that doesn't make you angry, please check your pulse. I remember having moments of rage at the thought of indignities I had faced and the opportunities I had been denied. How many times was I denied a job at which I could have excelled? How many times was I given a worse economic deal than someone in my same circumstance? How many other behind-the-scenes manipulations have occurred to keep me down while preferred others moved up? How many times had racism reached into my pocket and made withdrawals by the fistful? I was just as certain that I had been robbed of opportunity as I was certain the sun rose in the east and set in the west.

I've lived angry when I have had to explain this to people who live on the other side of the color line. How can they live in the same society as me and still not see it? How dare they suggest that I am making this up, or that I am overly sensitive, or that I am fighting a battle that has already been won? To borrow from America's founding fathers, we Black people hold this truth to be self-evident. Racism is alive and well. Racism is real because I have been past the mile markers, the recognition, shame, disappointment, and rage. I have felt its sting, the rage that accompanies losing opportunity (or worse) for no good reason.

I've lived angry, enraged by people in the media telling me that racism is over. It doesn't matter. Black people should simply get over it. Equality is already here, so I have no right to be angry. Oprah is proof that Black people have nothing left to complain about. If you do complain, you are just a lazy (fill-in-the-blank) who is ungrateful despite living in the greatest nation in the world.

I am tired of hearing the phrase, *"Racism still exists, but..."* from people who don't know racism from a hole in the ground. These people telling me they know racism is like me saying I know childbirth because I was in the delivery room twice watching it up close. I am wise enough to know that I don't know jack about childbirth. I am tired of people telling me how I am supposed to feel and how I am supposed to act.

I've lived angry when I heard other Blacks minimize the race issue or, even worse, take the wrong side of it. I have to admit that I have become unhinged when I have heard African Americans publicly argue the negative impact of racism is minimal or suggest that it no longer exists at all. More than once, hateful thoughts have crossed my mind. Hateful thoughts like, *"You treasonous (expletive deleted)! How can you fix your lips to minimize 'the struggle' in any way? All you did, to paraphrase Jack Nicholson in A Few Good Men, is weaken a Black nation today. All you did is add to our burden. Not only do I have to educate the uneducated on the topic of race, but now I need to explain away your dumb (expletive deleted) as well. You don't have to speak so loudly, Tom. Boss can't hear you now."*

And hateful thoughts like, *"And how in the world could anyone who calls themselves Black not support Barack Obama for president? Especially those who lived through the civil rights movement, how could you refuse to support him?*

I have seen films of sit-ins and protests, of brave people facing down attack dogs and fire hoses. I have read about so many people, well-known and unknown, martyred by the struggle, dying to support the simple idea that all men (and women) are created equal and should have the same rights under our American laws. Yet when we finally get a chance to vote for a Black person who could actually win the election, you choose to support someone else? When we are finally presented someone who embodies the Dream that inspired all of you to face those dogs, those hoses, the billy clubs, and the jack boots of some jacked-up redneck sheriff, you don't vote for him? Have you lost your (expletive deleted) mind?"

I have lived angry. My rage made me feel strong and powerful while I was raging, but it never delivered any strength or power that outlasted the rage. None of this "living angry" did me or us as a Black community any good. The only one who was ever hurt by my anger was me. My anger did not bring us even one half-step closer to realizing the Dream. Our anger does not help us win. Our anger only leaves us exposed to attack. It only provides proof that we are who "they" say we are. It only blinds us to real danger and confuses our analysis of real problems. It keeps us stuck in reverse, stuck on the set of the movie *Groundhog Day* living the same sorry day over and over again. It is time for a brand new day.

The Tie That Binds Us?

In so many ways, "living angry" is the tie that binds us African Americans together. It is the common language we all speak. At the start of the civil rights movement, the Black condition was, nearly universally, a common one. There was no such thing as an Oprah. A billionaire Black woman with seemingly limitless clout was a person who was not even conceivable. Even the great Willie Mays, centerfielder for the then-New York Giants, lived in the same neighborhood as the Blacks who idolized him. By and large, we were all in the same socio-economic class and products of the same set of experiences. We all rode at the "hind end" of the bus. Together, we transitioned from accepting a "separate but (un)equal" existence to becoming soldiers in a revolution that could no longer tolerate partial citizenship. As the dam held back the raging waters of equality gave way, so too broke the barrier that kept the Black condition a homogeneous one.

As we are painfully aware, most of us live in the United States today due to the African Diaspora caused by the trading of slaves. In the first two generations after the start of the civil rights movement, another diaspora (of sorts) has occurred. As a result of this diaspora, the African American experience is more varied today than it has ever been. Some people who call themselves "Black people" are among the richest and most powerful in the world and some are among the most destitute. Some Black people are graduates of the most prestigious schools in the world and some cannot read. Some have lived lives of extreme privilege and others live in extreme poverty. Some have many branches on their tree that are not African in descent at all. Like Barack Obama, some "African Americans" may not even have African American parents. There was a time when our largely uniform collective condition was enough to keep us together because our interests were naturally aligned. This is not the case any longer.

Today, living angry is sometimes the one single commonality we all share. It is the reason that a multi-millionaire athlete and a minimum wage earner can complain with equal veracity about the racism of their bosses and each can have sympathy for the other. In no other circumstance would a minimum wage earner have sympathy for the grievances of a multi-millionaire. We share laughs about living angry in comedy clubs and movie theaters all over the country. We can communicate with a short-hand about race that does not require any explanation, like a joke that requires no set up, but only the punch line. We empathize with each other when we hear stories of racism and lament over one more day of justice and equality denied. We allow each other our anger, our righteous indignation, with the knowledge that we have "been there" before as well and we fully expect to be there again. It is the one issue about which we can all relate when we have no other common ground. It is the reason we align ourselves on so many issues so overwhelmingly although we have never been more different from each other than we are today. It is the reason that a population as diverse in life experiences as is our Black community today can agree nearly unanimously on our choice of presidential candidate. Living angry is a tie that binds us together, perhaps serving as our strongest unifying force today.

But is this living angry also the tie that blinds us? Is it possible that our own thoughts about race are blinding us to the opportunities we have to succeed and, more importantly, our obligation to make it easier for our children to succeed? How often do we have to face real racism before we start expecting it, looking for it, and possibly seeing it when it is not there? How long will it be until we start accounting for racism to the point that we are discounting our own dreams for it?

We have already been taught to account for it. We all know that we have to work "twice as hard" and be "twice as good" to get to the same place as someone in the majority. But at what point does the expectation of racism and the failure it is supposed to bring start to affect our performance level or, even worse, our effort level? At what point do we start losing before racism even has a chance to beat us? At what point are we "doing ourselves" rather than "getting done" by some outside force?

Friends, I believe we are at that point. We are at the point at which we are doing as much to ourselves and blaming racism as racism is actually doing to us. We are at the point at which we must change our minds about living angry before we lose our minds altogether.

Getting Served

Sometimes anger feels good. It feels good to vent, to let it all out. It feels good to gather together with like-minded people and shout together and commiserate together. Nevertheless, we cannot mistake simply gathering and shouting for actually doing something. What has living angry gotten us? Perhaps jail time, broken hearts, and destroyed property, but nothing we actually wanted. Consider this. We are not the only ones who know racism is our trigger. This is the bait! You can bet those who oppose the best interests of Black people know our triggers as well as we do. They know that a good race issue provides a good distraction, a good subterfuge to divert our attention from more important matters. They know our anger always gets us to fall for the fake, leaving ourselves wide open for the long pass. Isn't it time we took that play out of their playbook? Is this anger serving us or have we just been "getting served?"

And if we are tired of being served, what will we decide to do differently? What will we do to fundamentally change the world in which we live today? What will our legacy be tomorrow? What is our version of the Civil Rights Act, the new Brown v. Board of Education? These are big questions which require big answers. I knew exactly who to ask for the big answers.

CHAPTER THREE
THE YSBs

There is no worse feeling than seeing someone you love in deep trouble. Loving someone makes you feel his or her pain like it's your own. Love hurts sometimes. When a loved one is in trouble, you don't sit idly by. You can't sit still at all. You just feel compelled to do something, say something, or even start writing a *Love Letter.* You will do anything you think will help because when someone you love is in trouble, you feel the pain. I love Black people. Black people are in deep trouble. I am feeling the pain.

Make no mistake about it. Black people are in deep trouble, although our trouble sometimes is masked by the exceptional accomplishments of the most accomplished among us. In fact, we are in the midst of an era of unprecedented success by the highest achieving Black people. We have broken down almost every door that was closed to us and we have racked up accomplishments that were unimaginable forty years ago. We have seen Black CEOs run some of the largest companies in the world. We have watched Oprah Winfrey become a billionaire and perhaps the most powerful person in the media industry. We have seen Tiger Woods simply take golf over and chart a course to become the first billionaire athlete. We have seen a Super Bowl winning coach and so many Blacks winning top honors at the Oscars that the racial significance of Forrest Whitaker's 2008 win for Best Actor barely made a blip. We have even seen two Black U.S. secretaries of State, Colin Powell and Condoleeza Rice, and both named to serve a Republican president. And, of course, we may be poised to elect our first Black president of the United States. If Barack wins this election, we will have progressed to the point where there will be no significant "firsts" left, and yet we will still be in deep trouble.

A Hurricane is Coming

We are not simply in trouble. We have a Katrina-sized, Category 5 hurricane barreling our way. Today, too many of our babies are having babies. Too many of our men and women are committing crimes. Too many of us are abusing drugs and alcohol. Too many of us are eating our way into early graves with adult-onset diabetes. In addition to our "African American specific" issues, we as part of the greater American society are subject to issues that are not unique to the Black community, like a recessionary economy, looming health care and energy crises, the potential bankruptcy of the Social Security system, and the global threat of terrorism. Without question, the average Black child born today is starting life in more difficult circumstances than did his or her parents. To say that Blacks in general are worse off today than a generation ago is no longer a matter for debate, but simply a statement of fact.

There are many urgent issues the Black community must face, but one stands out among the others. One problem truly warns of an impending catastrophe within the Black community. In fact, one single number is a symbol of everything that is wrong with the Black community, everything we must make right. That number is 53.4. This number is the percentage of Black high school students that graduated from high school during the 2003-2004 school year, as reported by the Editorial Projects in Education Research Center. Said differently, the likelihood that a Black child today will graduate from high school is barely better than the odds of correctly guessing the outcome of a coin flip. How in the world did we get here?

The graduation rate number itself is alarming, but the meaning of the number is downright scary. In an economy in which the price of entry for many of the least paying jobs is a high school diploma, almost 50 percent of our children of this age do not have the entry fee and therefore will be stuck on the lowest rung of the economic ladder. In an economy in which the price of a seat around a table at which decisions are made is no longer an undergraduate degree but a graduate degree, we are witnessing a generation of Black people who will not be decision makers but decision takers. Alone, our failure to educate our children puts the future of the Black community in serious jeopardy as every generation must eventually assume the role of leadership. However, when you consider perilous fates of non-high school graduates (higher crime and incarceration rates, higher teen pregnancy rates, higher drug abuse rates), the danger to our future increases exponentially. We are witness to a generation of Black children, perhaps the first generation, who could be considerably less accomplished than its parents. I hope this thought has you doubled over in pain as well.

Without question, this is a wrong we have to make right. We have to understand the mindset that delivered us here so we can reverse it. How did we go from fighting fiercely to ensure that every child received a high quality education to turning a blind eye as an alarming number of children fail to receive that education? What is the mindset that causes a child to "sign up" for a future of limited and mostly bad options? What is the mindset of a community, our Black community, which allowed it to happen? What will become of us when it is time for this generation to become our leaders, a generation we have failed so spectacularly?

For the answers, we should not look to our children, of course, but ourselves. Children come into this world as a clean slate. They have no fear, no cynicism, and acknowledge no limitation to their upside potential. They are born with an unlimited capacity to learn and an insatiable appetite for knowledge, as any parent who has answered the question "why?" posed by their young child twenty times consecutively can attest. Therefore, to the extent our children's fear of failure outstrips their will to win, we must take responsibility. To the extent our children have become too cynical to believe that hard work will deliver success, we must own this outcome as well. Our children are merely a reflection of the environment in which they were raised. To the extent that our children are sick, they carry an illness contracted from us.

No, it is no longer debatable whether our children inherited a tougher path to success than we did. They most certainly did. Here is the real debate. Is a Black community capable of being an agent of positive social change and positive economic impact on its way to extinction? Our biggest issue is not education rates, crime rates, or any other rate, but the mindset that allowed them all to occur. This is what we must fix. How do we fix that mindset, replacing it with one which has us running all out toward success rather than self-destruction? We ask a bunch of successful Black people to help us.

The Cavalry

We are in deep trouble, but I have good news. Help is on the way. However, the help will not come from traditional sources or by using traditional approaches. We will not get the help we need with a sit-in, a march, or a protest. We can lay our picket signs down for now. We can no longer look outside the Black community for help. Mainstream society does not see the race issue as an issue any longer or certainly not the issue, the burning platform whose fire must be extinguished immediately. The civil rights movement is over for the mainstream society and has been for quite some time.

Mainstream society has seen the successes of Oprah, Colin, Condi, and Barack. It sees these successful Blacks and many others as proof that the doors to success are wide open for Black people. In the minds of the mainstream, all the necessary legislation has been passed and all the necessary laws have been changed. If anything, mainstream society is starting to re-examine all of those laws to determine, in light of all this Black progress, whether they are now "obsolete." Strategies that make the same appeals that were ultimately successful in the 1960s will be utter failures today. Our largest issues no longer center on who to lobby or who to protest. There is no one left to "go see" about the freedom the Black community needs now, certainly no one outside the Black community. All of the "well-meaning outsiders" have seen Oprah, Colin, Condi, and Barack and wonder why there are not more of them. Don't you wonder too?

I have to admit that I like it this way. I don't want there to be anyone that we have to lobby or pressure or protest to get what we need to be successful. I don't want our fate to rest upon the benevolence of a group of politicians who don't have the same skin in the game as we do. The fact that there is no one left to "go see" is alright with me, because I am extremely uncomfortable with dependency. Aren't you? I don't like having to wait for someone else to make a decision on my behalf. I want to be a decision maker, someone who calls shots, not a decision taker, someone who responds to the shot called. I want us to control our destiny, so the fact that there is no one left to "go see" is good news to me.

The good news is that there is no need to wait for the cavalry. The help we need is not something we need someone else to allow us to do, but something we must allow ourselves to do. There is no need to wait for the cavalry because we are the cavalry. We are the change we are seeking in the Black community. Collectively, we have the answer to any and every problem with which we are faced.

The key word here is "collectively." There are countless members of the Black community who have cracked a part of the code, the riddle of being Black and successful in America. They have part of the answer as to how to be neither color-blind nor color-blinded. They know part of the secret of how to navigate around, over, and through the barriers to success, the barriers particular to Black people. Collectively, we have the answer. There are "code crackers" living all around us. They are you. They are us. The "help" that is on the way is the help we will give each other starting today. My fondest hope is that *Love Letter* will inspire you to offer and seek this help and to inspire others to do the same.

Getting this *Love Letter* "right" was too important to me for me to simply write it in a vacuum. There are too many of us who know something about success to allow our community to struggle like it does today. With this in mind, I gathered the opinions of more than one hundred successful Black people. Among this group were corporate executives, entrepreneurs, authors, educators, and civic leaders. They come from all corners of the country, different backgrounds, and different professional disciplines, but all are united in a common belief. They all love the Black community enough to share what they know in the hopes that we will all benefit. These successful Black people are just the tip of the iceberg, of course, regarding the knowledge we have to share with each other. We have many more "code crackers" among us than I was able to contact. No doubt you have the piece of the code as well, a piece that may make all the difference in the life of another brother or sister in the struggle. When we begin to share our knowledge more freely, we will be taking the first step toward becoming the difference makers I know we can be.

I was humbled and overwhelmed, but not at all surprised, by the support I was given by the Black community when I began *Love Letter.* I reached out to my network, my "patch in the quilt," sharing my intent to write "a *love letter* to Black people" and received more love in return than I could have ever imagined. The passion, the profound insight, and the love for the Black community that flowed so freely from those surveyed were deeply inspirational. *Love Letter* is my sincerest attempt to convey in words the inspiration I felt as I communicated with them and, through them, you.

Those who shared with me for *Love Letter* are merely a small subset of those who care deeply about the Black community. You are clearly one of these people. You are the success we dream about. You have the answers to all of our questions. You are those answers. You can and will change our future for the better through the strength of your determination and the love in your heart for the Black community, a love that led you to read a *Love Letter* to us.

For me, the most inspiring part of writing my letter to you was not receiving the inspirational advice of these successful Black people, which alone was life-changing. The most inspirational part of *Love Letter* for me was realizing the advice of these successful Black people, in all of its power and profundity, was an infinitesimally small representation of the power and knowledge our community holds in total.

I hope you will feel this power as I do. I hope, at this book's conclusion, you will feel as I do today. *Our future is in our hands and ours alone. We are a mighty people with an unlimited potential for success.*

Who are the "YSBs?"

Criteria of the Respondents (a.k.a. the "YSBs")

The YSBs surveyed for *Love Letter* fit the following criteria:

- **Black** – Those surveyed identify themselves as African-American. They feel the phrase "Black people" describes them.

- **Young** – Those surveyed are in their forties or younger. They are all products of the "post-civil rights" era, those who did not participate in the civil rights movement of the 1960s.

- **Successful** – Those surveyed are successful. For *Love Letter,* "successful" was defined as someone who is already accomplished in some regard (academic achievement, career achievement, or "overcoming"). Just as importantly, these YSBs believe themselves to be upwardly mobile in their careers and lives. They believe they will be even more accomplished, more successful "tomorrow" than they are today.

- **Not Celebrities** – Those surveyed are not famous. Most Blacks are not famous and never will be, yet so many do "their thing" so very well. These YSBs were selected to provide success strategies applicable to as wide a cross-section of Black people as possible.

- **Willing to Help** – Those surveyed were willing to share their opinions and to be quoted for the benefit of all who will read *Love Letter.*

Who are the YSBs?

If I was convinced of one thing as I began to write *Love Letter* it was that we, the Black community, held the keys to our future. We have so many people who are successful and Black that we could solve any problem by sharing our knowledge. We all have part of the answer to what ails us. My goal was to reach out to some of the many successful Black people among us for these answers. To that end, I had a specific type of person in mind with whom to make contact. The people whose brains I wanted to pick were young, successful, and Black, "YSBs" as I will refer to them going forward. More specifically, below is the definition of the people to whom I reached out and why I sought them in particular.

The YSBs are Black. All the YSBs identify themselves as African American. They believe the phrase "Black people" describes them. Of course, one of the best ways to learn how to do something is to ask someone who has already done it. Therefore, I sought people who "had done" successful and Black. Our YSBs face the same challenges we face as Black people, so they provide a natural starting point to learn how to "do success." I assumed they could give us tremendous insight on how to pursue and achieve success in the context of race and I was not disappointed.

The YSBs are young. All the YSBs are in their forties or younger. They are products of the "post-civil rights" era, people who did not participate in or live through the civil rights movement of the 1960s. I sought out "young" people for advice because I felt they would be more likely to see the world as it is and, more importantly, how it can be rather than how it was. It is not an accident that Dr. King was only twenty-six when he rose to prominence and Senator Barack Obama, if he is successful breaking the most significant glass ceiling remaining in America, would be one of the youngest presidents ever elected. History has proven over and over again that it is the young who create fundamental change in the world. It is the young who are idealistic enough to see a better future and passionate enough to battle the seemingly intractable forces of "the way things are." It is history's young that change the status quo.

If history is any guide, the "young" will be both our thought leaders and our action leaders.

The YSBs are successful. I did not wish to limit my definition of success to absolute terms (position, salary, particular achievements, a particular degree). I defined "successful people" more broadly to reflect my own personal beliefs regarding success. I believe that success occurs in the mind well before it manifests in the world. Muhammad Ali was calling himself "The Greatest" when the only belt he owned was the one holding up his pants. The successful Black people who were surveyed for *Love Letter* have an unwavering belief in their upward mobility in their careers and their personal lives. To be sure, all of the YSBs are all accomplished in some regard (be it academic achievement, career achievement, or simply in "overcoming"). More significantly, however, they all have no doubt that they will be even more accomplished, more successful "tomorrow" than they are today. They have the "right mind" for success and, therefore, they are excellent resources from which to learn.

The YSBs are not celebrities. My intent by limiting the group in this way was not to exclude anyone, but to build a message that has the widest practical application possible. Simply by the nature of our society, Blacks who become celebrities are no longer subject to the same "rules" when it comes to race. I remember the great scene in Spike Lee's *Do the Right Thing* in which two white brothers, one racially tolerant and one just plain racist, were having a discussion about race. The racially tolerant brother asked the racist brother to name his favorite athletes and celebrities, questions to which the racist brother offered names of Black celebrities as his answers. The tolerant brother then asked the racist one how he could have so many Black favorites while harboring so much animosity toward the Blacks in his own neighborhood. The racist brother, without a hint of sarcasm, replied, "They (the celebrities) aren't Black."

Of course, most Blacks are not famous and never will be. As a result, they have to live in a different racial environment than do Black celebrities. Further, most of our Black celebrities become successful in fields accustomed to seeing Black success. The YSBs surveyed have achieved their success by playing by the same rules and facing the same constraints that the majority of Blacks face. In many cases, they have had to blaze trails where there were none. Therefore, they have a great deal of knowledge that is practical to the vast majority of us.

The YSBs are willing to help. They were not motivated by the prospect of reward for offering their advice. As I contacted each one of them, I told them that I was writing "a love letter to Black people" and they all jumped at the chance to share their knowledge out of love for the Black community. In many cases, they led me to other success minded Black people like themselves who were equally willing to share their knowledge. In so doing, they modeled the behavior that has been the foundation of every group that ever enjoyed success. They offered the first "answer" before any question was asked. Through their participation in *Love Letter,* the YSBs demonstrated their love for the Black community first by putting their desire to help above any potential personal gain.

I found the opinions of this group of YSBs to be passionate, thoughtful, enlightening, profound, and often inspirational. They were all fiercely optimistic about the future, both their futures and that of the Black community, despite the sometimes daunting challenges we face. Every day, they demonstrate the same audacious hopefulness as the man who plans to become the first Black president of the United States. In fact, my "Obama Epiphany" is not an epiphany at all to a great many African Americans. Many Blacks are already living according to the Obama success blueprint. They are already living Black without being defined (or confined) by being Black. They are already authoring a new definition of what it means to be successful and Black. They have already begun to free their minds of outdated views regarding race and success, and this freedom has helped to accelerate their success. They are already working to ensure our children will live with minds even more free than their own. Through their good works, they share their own love letters with all with whom they come in contact.

Questions Asked of the YSBs

1. *What role has race played in your past and current success?* In other words, how has race aided or inhibited your pursuit of success.

2. *What role do you expect race to play in your future success?* In other words, how do you expect race to aid or inhibit your future success.

3. Some successful Blacks have been praised as "staying Black" or "keeping it real" while others have been condemned as "sellouts," "acting white," or even as "race traitors." *Do you believe that there is a "right" way to succeed as an African-American? If so, how so? If not, why not?*

4. *To what extent do you tailor your behavior personally, politically, or professionally out of a sense of responsibility to the larger Black community?*

5. *What advice would you give to the aspiring YSBs? What should they start or continue doing? What should they stop doing?*

The Questions Posed to the YSBs

If you don't know, you better ask somebody. What did I ask these YSBs? How they do it, of course. I was very curious to know how they would explain their ability to conquer racism to the degree they had. I wanted to know why they believe they are successful when many Blacks do not enjoy that same level of success. Before starting *Love Letter*, I did not believe these YSBs were just lucky or fortunate but that they helped make their own luck through the way they viewed the challenges presented by being Black. I believed these YSBs were successful, at least in part, because they viewed their race in a way that aided their success. To that end, I selected five questions intended to uncover how each YSB approached his or her success as it pertained to race.

Question 1 - What role has race played in your past and current success? In other words, how has race aided or inhibited your pursuit of success.

I was particularly interested in how the YSBs viewed the racism in their lives and how they conquered it. Did they have special strategies they employed to counter racism from which we could learn? Did they seek situations in which racism would be less of a factor, thus putting themselves in a better position to succeed? Were they simply fortunate individuals who simply found themselves in better situations than those who were more negatively impacted by racism? Do they view their environment in such a way that leaves them better equipped to deal with racism? Most likely "the answer" has elements of all of the above. Nonetheless, I was curious to see if there were consistent themes that would connect their answers.

Question 2 – What role do your expect race to play in your future success?

I have already written that these YSBs were chosen for their unwavering belief in their ability to succeed, so I did not expect any of them to say that racism would prevent them from being successful. However, I was curious to see to what extent they expected to "game plan" for racism in the future. Therefore, this question was intended to help understand their keys to acquiring and maintaining their success mindset.

Question 3 - Do you believe that there is a "right" way to succeed as an African-American? If so, how so? If not, why not?

The context of this question was very important. I prefaced it by letting the YSBs know that I was asking them to comment on the notion of "acting white" and "selling out." Some successful Blacks receive praise for "staying Black" or "keeping it real" while others receive condemnation as "sellouts," "acting white," or even as "race traitors." Unfortunately, we Black people are responsible for erecting some of the barriers we face to being successful. The aspersion "acting white" or "selling out" is often used as a wedge by Blacks against other Blacks. By asking this question, I hoped to gain insight as to how these YSBs avoid being wounded by "friendly fire" or, at least, recover quickly from the wounds.

Question 4 - To what extent do you tailor your behavior personally, politically, or professionally out of a sense of responsibility to the larger Black community?

The presumption that is made by Blacks who suggest others are guilty of "race treason" is that there is a "right way" to be successful and Black. Presumably, there are some activities in which Blacks should never engage regardless of the potential for individual gain because they are too detrimental to the Black community as a whole. In general, most Blacks believe that Blacks should not pursue success to the detriment of the larger Black community. However, it is far from clear how we should define this notion of "detriment." If there is a wrong way to be successful, which activities should appear on the "banned list?" As I asked Question 4, the questions beneath the question were these: How did the YSBs separate the "right" success from the "wrong" success? Did they believe in this notion at all? Did the YSBs feel their actions, or ours, should be governed in some way by the wishes of the Black community? Would they look to the Blacks in their lives for advice regarding the "responsible way" to be successful? My hope was that the answers to these questions could reduce the divisiveness among members of the Black community.

Question 5 - What advice would you give to the aspiring "YSBs?" What should they start or continue doing? What should they stop doing?

I could not pass up the opportunity to further pick the brains of the YSBs by asking them the "success question" directly. Any successful person will tell you that associating with successful people will hasten your success. Therefore, I am looking to hasten our success as a Black community by associating us with all of these YSBs at once.

What Will We Learn From the YSBs?

What will we learn from the YSBs? In a word, love. The YSBs live their lives governed by love. These YSB, and YSBs everywhere, love themselves as individuals enough to get out of their own way. From their advice, we can learn how they avoid adding to the challenges we already face as African Americans by refusing to succumb to the self-sabotage of irrational fears or counterproductive self-doubt regarding race. We can learn how to love our greatness more than we fear its price and therefore become well-equipped to navigate the sometimes jagged path to success. *Love Letter* will discuss how we African Americans can stay focused on success when "the evidence" suggests otherwise.

Further, YSBs love the Black community enough to put it first. Through their words, these YSBs collectively suggest a success approach that demonstrates a love for the Black community and a responsibility to it. *Love Letter* will discuss how we can all demonstrate this "responsibility" to the Black community for our collective benefit. The YSBs were especially passionate about how we Black people relate to one another today and how our relationship must change to enable our success.

Finally, the YSBs will suggest how we can embody the love message for the sake of future generations. We will decide today how our children carry the weight of racism. We will decide whether our children will still wait for the cavalry to save them or choose to become the cavalry. Our ability or inability to deliver this love message to our children will decide whether they will have a clear vision of the greatness the Black community can enjoy or whether we will risk another generation of debilitating "color-blindedness." The central message of these YSBs is the reason this book is titled *Love Letter*. We can, we must, and we will love our way to greatness as a Black community. It is our only hope.

CHAPTER FOUR
CARRYING THE WEIGHT

You will have to work twice as hard to achieve the same success.
– Commonly Held Belief

I don't know one Black person who was not taught the "twice as hard" lesson as a child. Do you? Even today, many Black parents would consider it irresponsible, an act of parental malpractice, to raise a child without ingraining in that child an appreciation for the "twice as hard" lesson. This is what parents are supposed to do. Parents are supposed to make their children aware of life's dangers, instilling a healthy amount of fear in their children to prepare them for the hard realities of life. Hot stoves burn hands, long falls break necks, and racism breaks dreams (at least some of them). Our parents felt it was imperative to teach us that the rules which applied to us and those which applied to the majority were often two very different sets of rules. The "twice as hard" lesson often translated to "your life will be 'twice as hard' as the life of your majority counterpart." Our parents taught us this lesson out of responsibility to us, out of love. They taught us to expect racism because failing to do so could put us squarely in harm's way. At one point in our nation's history, ignorance of the "race rules" was fatal.

The story of Emmitt Till is perhaps the most famous story illustrating the dire consequences of being ignorant of the "race rules." Emmitt Till was a fourteen-year-old boy who was murdered for allegedly whistling at a white woman in rural Mississippi in 1955. Till was in Mississippi visiting relatives for the summer and was unaware that, unlike in his hometown of Chicago, his playful whistle was a "capital offense." After news of Till's whistle spread throughout that Mississippi town, he was abducted, beaten, and shot to death. Later, his murderers tied a seventy-five pound weight to his body and dropped it to the bottom of the Tallahatchie River. After Till's body was recovered, his mother elected to have an open casket funeral to put the utter savagery of the murder on full display. Justice? The murderers (as proven by subsequent confessions) were arrested and stood trial, but were acquitted by an all-white male jury that took a mere sixty-seven minutes to deliberate. The case of Emmitt Till is often placed among the key events that sparked the civil rights movement. This case also helped burn an image in two generations of minds that racism is not something with which to be trifled.

With full knowledge of Emmitt Till and the many other examples of "race rules" ignorance gone wrong, our parents taught us to prepare for the inevitable sting of racism. In the business world, we were taught to expect to work harder and get less than our non-Black peers. We were taught to expect to have our passion misconstrued as aggression and our dissent as hostility. We were taught that succeeding in a corporate environment meant conforming to the prevailing culture.

In mainstream society, we were taught to expect our intelligence, our motives, and our integrity to be questioned. We were taught to assume that society would view us as under-educated and ill-informed and, therefore, discount or disregard our opinions. Society would assume we were more prone to violence, so our mere presence would make some people uneasy. We would be assumed to be criminal-minded, so our movements would be scrutinized more closely than those of non-Blacks. We were taught to expect no benefit of the doubt if we were to enter the legal system. Our parents believed that if we understood all of this, we would be better equipped to make the choices and take the actions necessary to get along in the "white man's world." For most Blacks, these lessons are as familiar as A-B-C and 1-2-3.

Today, the "twice as hard" lesson is practically part of our DNA. This lesson has been taught so well that we no longer require real life examples in order to fortify the lesson. Typically, a child will not believe a stove is hot until he or she feels the burn one time. Today, we often believe in the burn of racism without having been burned ourselves. Black Ivy League graduates, despite receiving a six-figure education followed by a six-figure income, decry the opportunities they have been denied in their lives. Black suburban kids drive their parents' Benzes to school, and then complain about the "overseer" who denied them a hall pass. I do not write this to criticize those who appear advantaged but still feel aggrieved. A problem is always a relative thing. If you want to get bent out of shape about the temperature of the silk sheets that drape the king-sized mattress on your brass canopy bed, that is, as Bobby Brown sang, your Prerogative. However, there is a larger question. Have we taught and been taught the "twice as hard" lesson too well? Does expecting racism to this degree serve us today?

"The Man"

"They" will never let a Black man/woman (fill in the blank).
– Commonly held belief

"They" will always keep us down. Isn't this the logical conclusion to be drawn from the "twice as hard" lesson? If the game is rigged against us, then it's reasonable to believe those rigging the game will not allow us to win at anything important. In fact, they may want to do us harm out of pure malice or to advantage themselves in some way. We all know this has happened in the past. "The Man" himself, in the form of the U.S. federal government, has acknowledged this fact on any number of occasions. Perhaps none of these acknowledgements were more shocking than the revelation of the Tuskegee Study of Untreated Syphilis in the Negro Male, also known as the Tuskegee Experiment.

The Tuskegee Experiment was a study for which 399 poor Black men who were thought to have syphilis were recruited by scientists for the purpose of studying the effects of the disease on humans when left untreated. The study, which was performed at Tuskegee University in Tuskegee, Alabama, was conducted from 1932 until 1972 and only ended after the news of its existence was leaked to the public.

Despite the emergence of penicillin as the common treatment for syphilis by 1947, the study steadfastly stuck to its objective of observing the damage syphilis exacted on human patients up until death and studying them post-mortem. By the end of the study, only seventy-four of the original 399 survived, with 128 dying directly of syphilis or related complications. In addition, at study's end, forty of these men passed their syphilis to their wives and nineteen children had been born with congenital syphilis.

There are no words to adequately describe what took place at Tuskegee, but I will choose the word "shocking" as a proxy for a more adequate description. The Tuskegee Experiment was shocking due to the length of time it was conducted and the era in which it was conducted. This study ended twenty-five years after the end of the Nuremburg Trials in which Nazi medical doctors were put to death for their roles in human experiments on Jewish concentration camp prisoners. The Tuskegee Experiment continued for eighteen years after Brown v. the Board of Education, eight years after the Civil Rights Act, and four years after the assassination of Dr. King. The study was shocking for where it was performed, at the university founded by legendary African American educator Booker T. Washington. The study was shocking for its wonton disregard for human life, its clinical cruelty, and the vehement protestations of its leaders, who argued even after the end of the study that such inhumanity was justified. The Tuskegee Experiment was shocking by any and every standard imaginable, even to a people accustomed to sub-standard treatment. It left a mark on our African American psyche that we are not even close to removing.

The most damaging legacy of the Tuskegee Experiment is that it breathed new life into the concept of "The Man," a concept that could have lost its footing after the dramatic progress made by Blacks in the 1960s. Given the revelation of the Tuskegee Experiment, is there any wonder some Blacks believe any number of conspiracy theories, no matter how far-fetched they may appear? After Tuskegee, it is not difficult for many Blacks to believe HIV was created in a U.S. government laboratory and willfully injected into Black people to thin our ranks. After Tuskegee, it is not difficult for many Blacks to believe that the advent of crack cocaine and the corresponding heavier sentences for its use was not a "perfect storm" which befell the Black community but a declaration of war on the Black community. Some Blacks even believe that birth control is simply a trick to keep Blacks from procreating and even gangsta rap is really one big, carefully orchestrated program of self-sabotage guided by the malevolent hand of "The Man." After Tuskegee, can we blame anyone who ascribes to any or all of the above?

Even with full knowledge of the Tuskegee Experiment, most of us do not believe in the most nefarious of these conspiracy theories. Most of us do not believe in the existence of "The Man," an actual all-knowing, all-seeing, success preventing, anti-Black organization. However, I would argue that a great many of us believe in the concept of "The Man." To many of us, "The Man" does live in the structural racism which permeates American society, the slanted playing field we face in so many facets of our lives. Many of us do view the world through race-colored glasses.

Some of this cannot be avoided because as humans we are all products of our environments. Is it unreasonable to recall our past when trying to interpret our present or plan for our future? Is it unreasonable? No. Is it dangerous? Yes.

It may be reasonable to look to the past to explain or even predict the future, but it is also very dangerous. A backward-looking attitude or approach can do extreme violence to our prospects for future success. Greatness by definition is an extraordinary, sometimes unprecedented, achievement. At its most basic level, greatness starts with the belief in something that cannot be proven will be successful. The effort that greatness requires will only be put forth by someone who believes that effort is not in vain. Therefore, greatness can only be achieved by a believer, someone who believes that his or her greatness, even if unprecedented, is possible. The ramifications of the power of belief for the Black community are profound. If we believe the game is inexorably rigged, how can we believe in our ability to succeed at anything? Said differently, is it possible for the Black community to believe in "The Man" and our own potential for greatness at the same time?

Anyone who says that being Black, all else being equal, is harder than being in the majority is "right" in the sense that there is ample evidence to support that assertion. Anyone who feels angry about the poor treatment they or their people have received due to race has a grievance, a legitimate grievance. However, being "right" is not necessarily a good thing. Believing that your upside is capped is harmful to your success dreams at best and fatal to those dreams at worst. Does wondering whether the hiring manager interviewing you is a racist make you more likely to get the job? Does believing that Black public figures are in more danger than white ones because some people hate Blacks enough to kill help you do anything productive? Does looking for the "racial explanation" for every situation make us as a people more likely to succeed? Does the constant acknowledgement of the weight of racism make the weight easier for us to carry or does it simply weigh us down?

Searching for Racism

Racism is the reason Blacks fail. To explain the failure, find the racism.
– Commonly Held Belief

This is a dangerous belief for us to hold because one can always establish a link between the manifestations of racism and the plight of so many in our Black community. It is easy to connect the dots between slavery and Jim Crow and the failure of Blacks to get a quality education or to build intergenerational wealth. If you were to focus on home lending practices alone, you would find that Blacks have historically found it more difficult to get loans and were charged more for them for no other reason than being Black. You can analyze the historical trends in any number of areas and discover the same discouraging results. The evidence is clear. But does this knowledge help us succeed tomorrow? How many years must pass before we stop mapping everything back to slavery and Jim Crow and using it as sufficient justification of a present that is unacceptable? At what point should we decide to move forward despite the evidence? "Yesterday" may provide a partial explanation for today, but we cannot allow it to be an excuse for what happens tomorrow.

Believing in the grand conspiracy has an even more insidious effect than simply dampening our efforts toward success. Believing in a malevolent hand that discourages Black achievement also requires that one believes Black people are simple-minded enough to cooperate with "the hand." I think too highly of Black people to believe we are this simple. I know you feel the same way. I refuse to believe we are gullible enough to fall for the equivalent of the banana in the tailpipe, as were the cops tailing Eddie Murphy in *Beverly Hills Cop*. I refuse to believe that someone, anyone, can create a CD so hot that it will force us to abandon our own free will. I refuse to believe that a Black community that has demonstrated such strength for so long is that weak-minded today. I refuse to believe that we are that easily manipulated.

When met with the expectation of racism, there are only two reactions we can have. This expectation of racism will provide motivation or de-motivation. It will be part of the reason why we choose to succeed or our ready-made excuse for failure. Some people will take the message, "they are against you" and pour every ounce of effort they have into defeating "they." So many of the Black super-achievers we admire can trace their success back to a slight that sparked their desire to be great. That slight caused them to pay the price of greatness by doing the work of greatness. But paying this price and doing this work was only possible because these Black super-achievers refused to believe in the power of "they." By doing the work of greatness, these super-achievers declared, "They cannot stop me" and then proved themselves right.

They may have been motivated by "The Man," but clearly they did not believe in "his" omnipotence.

Unfortunately, too many Blacks take the "they" message at face value. When you think about it, the ones that heed the message are acting more logically than the super-achievers. If you woke up one morning and heard on the radio that the route you had planned to drive to work was impassable, you would automatically choose a different route, right? So what should you do if you hear with regularity that your route in life is "impassable?" If you truly believe "they" will make all routes to success impassable, you must choose failure. Unfortunately, this is the choice that too many of us make. Why study in school? "They" will not let me graduate. Why graduate? "They" will not hire me. Why work hard? "They" will not promote me. You get the point. Again, this is not an unreasonable conclusion if you believe in the awesome power of "they" as we have been taught.

However, believing in the power of "they" is a completely unacceptable conclusion if we desire to grow more successful as a Black community. This conclusion wrongly chooses to remember our failures and deny our many successes. This conclusion ignores the fact that, although we do not win as much as we should, we do win quite frequently. We are at the point in our history where we must choose. We have to choose to believe in an all-powerful "they" or in our power as a people. We cannot believe in both.

I know you know there is no reason for Black people to believe in an all-powerful "they." There are too many living examples of our awesome power for us to believe we have no power. However, our challenges as a people demonstrate that we are not as powerful as we can be. Too often, we cede our power to self-destructive thoughts of "they." We get distracted, confounded, and ultimately defeated by thoughts of "they." I asked our YSBs about "they" and the extent to which racism has impacted their past and present successes. I expected to hear coping strategies, actions they had taken to defeat racism. I expected to hear wistful stories of opportunities lost as they proudly recounted all they had achieved. I expected to hear a variety of ways in which we could beat "they," a consistent pattern from which we could learn.

There was a consistent pattern to answers our YSBs gave to this question, but it was not quite the pattern I expected.

CHAPTER FIVE
"THE MAN" IS DEAD

Conventional Black wisdom says that being Black in America is a net negative. It offers more bad than good. No matter how much success a Black person enjoys, that person would have had more success had he or she not been born Black. And because the only certainties in our Black lives are that we will "stay Black and die," conventional Black wisdom dictates that we must simply accept our Black burden.

Those who ascribe to this conventional Black wisdom can draw upon countless situations in which Blacks were disadvantaged for no reason but being Black to bolster this belief. To the supporters of conventional Black wisdom, "The Man" is still very much alive and well. They argue the proper response to "The Man" is to remain vigilant in tracking his every movement and vocal in publicizing his whereabouts at all occasions. However, I have news for the proponents of the conventional Black wisdom. Truly successful Blacks do not believe in conventional Black wisdom or an outside force named "The Man."

"The Man" is Dead!

"The Man" is dead! This was the emphatic response from our YSBs when asked, "What role has your race played in your past and current success? How has race aided or inhibited your pursuit of success?" These YSBs stated without equivocation that they did not believe in the existence of a nefarious force strong enough to prevent their success. Successful Black people understand "The Man" is not an individual, a group of individuals, or some aspect of an unseen power structure. "The Man" is an embodiment of the self-doubt we invite into our minds, the negative impact of which we later attribute to racism. You are "The Man." Read this sentence again. YOU are "The Man." "The Man" is not an external force, but a force that lives inside every one of us to some degree, an inner voice we must work fiercely every day to silence. When we begin to silence this inner voice, we may begin to commit ourselves completely to success.

The most successful Blacks among us are absolutely unwilling to submit to the notion of "The Man" in any way. They will not concede that their failures are predetermined by their race or that their successes can be prevented in any way by discrimination or intolerance. They believe that making any such concession would rob them of the power they feel over their own lives, and powerful people do not cede power willingly. These successful Blacks fight these mental chains as fiercely as our slave ancestors fought the physical ones. Therefore, they choose freedom and the responsibility of this freedom. They understand that discrimination and intolerance may sometimes detour their path to success, but they can never deter it without their permission.

Quieting the inner voice of self-doubt and enjoying the resultant freedom requires courage. Quieting this voice consistently is an act of courage because in declaring one's emancipation from "The Man," he or she must also accept full responsibility for the outcome of his or her life. Once you accept the responsibility and the blame for your life, then and only then do you have the power to change it. This requires an act of courage because it is human nature to rationalize away poor results. In fact, a person's ability to rationalize his or her own failures is infinite. Successful Black people have the courage to own their failures wholeheartedly, but with the knowledge they can makes them into successes. With no one else to blame, these successful Black people place the onus on themselves to find "a way" from "no way." More often than not, they find a way. Rejecting "The Man" takes courage because it requires us to live life without a safety net set to catch all of our failures. Black people, we do not need this net. There are no more courageous people on Earth than we.

Throwing Off the Yoke

We are courageous enough to reject "The Man," and we must. Believing in any force outside our control that we can blame for our failures is tantamount to giving ourselves permission to fail. With permission to fail, each instance of failure becomes that much more palatable and living with enduring failure becomes that much more acceptable. Social scientists call the phenomenon "learned helplessness." Learned helplessness is defined as a *"psychological condition in which a human being or an animal has learned to act or behave helpless in a particular situation, even when it has the power to change its unpleasant or even harmful circumstances."* In 1967, psychologists Martin Seligman and Steve Maier performed an experiment that demonstrated this condition.

In the Seligman and Maier experiment, three groups of dogs were placed in harnesses. The dogs in Group One were simply placed in harness for a period of time and then released. Group Two and Group Three dogs were placed in harnesses and yoked together in pairs (one dog from Group Two with one dog from Group Three) and exposed to electric shocks. In the experiment, each pair of dogs was exposed to the same electric shock but only one dog in the pair had the ability to end the shock. The dogs in Group Two could end the shock by pressing a lever, but the dogs in Group Three had a lever which did not impact the shock. The shock ended for a Group Three dog only when the dog with which it was paired in Group Two pressed its lever. Therefore, the dogs in Group Three believed the shock ended at random and learned to believe they were helpless to end the shock. The dogs were observed further after the experiment. The dogs in Group One and Group Two quickly recovered from the experiment, but the dogs in Group Three exhibited lingering depression-like effects.

Seligman and Maier performed a second part of the experiment in which the dogs from all three groups were placed in a new apparatus and again exposed to electric shocks. The dogs could escape the shock by jumping over a low partition. The overwhelming majority of dogs in Groups One and Two from the first part of the experiment easily escaped the shock. However, two-thirds of the dogs from Group Three in the first experiment lay down and accepted the shock in the second part of the experiment. They had retained the belief that they were helpless.

Believing in the irresistible power of "The Man" is no different than lying down to accept our shock. It is the same as accepting that being Black is a hopeless, helpless condition. When we accept that we are helpless to prevent failure, we will ourselves into poor performance. This expectation of failure becomes the self-fulfilling prophesy that we have seen manifest on countless occasions. Be it the athlete in a slump who expects to miss her next shot because she missed her last several or the child who expects to fail his test because he believes he is not smart enough to pass, those who expect a negative outcome usually get one.

Believing in "The Man," the all-powerful "they," is tantamount to becoming comfortable with losing. No one who is comfortable with chronic losing will ever win consistently. Winning requires a consistent hunger for winning and a consistent effort toward winning. At the moment that losing becomes comfortable, it becomes inevitable. We have to resist this urge to lie down in the face of the shock. Believing we are helpless in the face of "The Man" has caused us to run at half-speed (or not at all) toward our success in life. In this regard, we must learn from the successful Blacks who have learned to take the shocks of racism differently and teach others to do the same.

We are not like these dogs. We do not have to accept that failure is our fate. We are not destined to drop out of school, to commit violent crimes on one another, to become teenaged parents, or to abuse drugs. None of this is our fate, so we should not accept it as given. Failing to have the success we desire in life is not fated to us either. We need to make no concession in our lives for being Black. NONE! We are a powerful people. We have complete ownership over our circumstances. We will not allow anyone else to even see the deed to our dreams, let alone hold it or control it in any way. We must throw off the yoke. This is what you must tell "The Man" the next time you see him.

Twice as Hard? – The Wrong Message

Most of us do not actually walk through life believing our success will be thwarted at every turn. Even the most ardent believers in "The Man" allow themselves hope once in a while. However, because "The Man" lives inside us, he often appears at the most inopportune times. Often we succumb to subtle forms of expecting failure, just enough to plant a seed of doubt that will become a redwood if we are not careful. Too often our response to a negative outcome is to search for the racism in the situation, seeking solace in the notion that our failure was foretold and, therefore, not our fault. We tell ourselves that if we win, "we did it," but if we lose, "he did it." This attitude does not allow us to win consistently because we always have a comfortable excuse for losing.

Ultimately even the "twice as hard" lesson is the wrong lesson for Blacks to teach or internalize today because it assumes a level of helplessness. The "twice as hard" lesson is a tacit understanding that there are situations in which we will not be allowed to win, situations in which we are helpless and should expect to fail. We can never expect to fail. Anything that is man-made, as is racism, can be man-conquered or man-destroyed. We shouldn't try to motivate each other with helplessness. This is the wrong message, a mixed message that will miss the mark as often as it hits it.

If effort is what we seek to inspire, there are many better ways than the "twice as hard" lesson. We should teach each other to work hard because hard work delivers excellence. We should work hard to bring honor to our families, our friends, our school, our city, or whomever or whatever else we represent. We should work hard because the Black community requires our best effort so it may be more successful. We should work hard for hard work's own sake. But we should not work hard because racism requires it. The "twice as hard" lesson is an insidious form of "Man-worship" that we must also reject. The most successful Blacks among us do not engage in self-doubt, allowing themselves an explanation for failure, an excuse which assigns the blame for failure elsewhere. It prevents 100 percent accountability, and they live their lives powerfully with 100 percent accountability. In fact, none of us in the Black community should legitimize self-doubt by looking for reasons to believe in "The Man." The best parts of our history have been marked by the successes of Black people who would not take "no" for an answer. The Black people we most admire were certifiably uncomfortable with anything less than overwhelming success. Where would we be today if Harriet Tubman thought that saving herself was enough success? What if Dr. King, rather than writing *Why We Can't Wait,* wrote *Why We Can Wait Just a Little While Longer?* They made no concessions for being Black and never wallowed in self-doubt. Very much to the contrary, they believed that our goals were righteous and the victory of righteousness was inevitable. They believed the righteous simply had to make it so. They had to do the work. Those whose shoulders upon which we stand today first disavowed the notion that their failure was preordained, and then they went to work to bring about this success. In this spirit, we must continue the work today with their spirit that anything less than success is intolerable.

If we are to become a greater, more successful people, then we must replace our belief in "The Man" with a belief in ourselves, accepting full credit and full blame for the outcomes in our lives. This does not mean that we should deny that racism exists or ignore injustice rather than battle it. However, we must, as have the successful Blacks we must emulate, find the balance between being color-blind and color-blinded. We must value winning despite racism more than we value being "right" about racism. We must get so uncomfortable with the "moral victories" but "actual losses" that we can't sleep. We must refuse to be graded on a curve by accepting a less stringent definition of success and therefore aspiring to a lower level of achievement.

We must always refuse to be judged by a lower standard of achievement because, by accepting this lower standard, we confirm to the world that we are, in fact, an inferior group of people. We confirm that we are incapable of better and therefore we need the world's charity. We confirm that we can be controlled by "The Man," that we are willing to give "him" power over our lives and responsibility for them. We confirm that we are willing to leave it in his hands. "He" can decide how successful "he" wants us to be. Worst of all, we confirm all of these notions to ourselves. We cannot afford to believe in our own inferiority even in the smallest of ways.

When we choose to believe in "The Man," we are agreeing that we are inferior and we are agreeing to stay inferior. I hope, in your heart of hearts, you cannot and will not agree. I hope you find the thought of giving up power and control of your life repugnant. I hope the thought smells like hot garbage and tastes like spoiled milk to you. I hope the whole notion makes you angry enough…to choose love. The successful Blacks we must emulate choose to believe in love. They love their own greatness more than they fear its price. So can we all.

Powerful Beyond Measure

Sadly, even in 2008, racism is inevitable. However, our response to it is not. We must not add to the weight of racism with the self-sabotage of allowing the existence of racism to impact the effort we put forth. We must not spend so much time trying to prove the game is rigged that we fail to study those Blacks who unrigged the game and apply the lessons learned. Every rigged game can be unrigged when we pay close enough attention to the way the game is played and the motivations of the players. This requires us to focus on winning the game rather than lamenting how difficult the game is.

How can we acquire this focus? We can learn much from our YSBs (those surveyed for *Love Letter* and the countless others out there doing their thing) on this count. They are the embodiment of the sentiment so artfully written by Marianne Williamson in Our Deepest Fear.

Our deepest fear is not that we are inadequate.
Our deepest fear
is that we are powerful beyond measure.
It is our light, not our darkness,
that most frightens us.
We ask ourselves, who am I to be brilliant, gorgeous,
talented and fabulous?
Actually who are we not to be?
You are a child of God.
Your playing small doesn't serve the world.
There is nothing enlightened about shrinking
so that other people
won't feel insecure around you.
We are all meant to shine as children do.
We were born to make manifest
the glory of God that is within us.
It's not just in some of us; it's in everyone.
And when we let our own light shine,
we unconsciously give other people
permission to do the same.
As we are liberated from our own fear,
our presence automatically liberates others.

I am powerful beyond measure. This is the mindset with which our YSBs, and successful Blacks everywhere, attack the challenges they face on a daily basis. They love themselves too much to accept failure as their destiny. They love themselves enough to know they deserve success, so they put themselves in the best possible position to claim it. They love themselves enough to demand the freedom to choose their fates rather than leaving this decision to others. They believe in love. Do you?

These YSBs do not consider themselves to be a special group of people on whom racism has no power. They have simply declared independence from the self-destructive thinking that so often creates doubt and frustration in our minds rather than solutions and accomplishments. They have simply adopted a love mindset which allows them to succeed or, better yet, drives their success. Part of this mindset is to declare "The Man" deceased. As it pertains to race and success, these YSBs access their power beyond measure as described on the following pages. YSBs take one of the following approaches to ensure "The Man," the self-doubt we attribute to racism, stays dead.

"Being Black is an advantage"

Sports teams consistently win more often in their home stadium than in the stadiums of their opponents. Statistics have shown in sport after sport and season after season that home teams "over-perform" at home and "under-perform" away from home. Why is this true? Some of the explanation lies in the comforts of home. The players on the home team sleep in their own beds the night before the event, eat home cooking before they leave for the stadium, and find familiar surroundings when they get there. They are comfortable, as are we all, at home.

However, this difference in performance goes far beyond simply being comfortable. Players on the home team have heard the same stories and read the same statistics as the fans. They know they are supposed to have an advantage at home. Emboldened by this knowledge, they simply perform better. They are more encouraged and draw more confidence when the game is going well and less discouraged when they game is not going well. Why? They know they have are supposed to have an advantage, so they will their performance to make that advantage a reality. They are successful because they feel they are supposed to be successful. Most of the time, success is a state of mind before it is a manifestation of results.

What if you went through life believing you had an advantage? If you went through life expecting to win, believing you were supposed to win, you would react differently to the game too. You would gain confidence from the positive outcomes in your life and be less discouraged by the negative ones. After all, you have an advantage, right? The mental advantage players on the home team enjoy has nothing to do with the game on the field and everything to do with the game between their ears. They choose to believe they have an advantage and the advantage manifests in results year after year in sport after sport.

Many successful Black people, including some surveyed for *Love Letter,* believe that being Black has given them an advantage in life. They are emboldened by the positive reinforcement of that notion, affirmative action, or other situations where being Black is tangibly beneficial, and they are less discouraged in cases where being Black is not a benefit. Some YSBs even attribute traits that are not necessarily race-specific, like determination or perseverance, to being Black. If we have to "stay Black and die," why shouldn't we view being Black as an advantage? Won't believing you are supposed to win make you play better? Many YSBs say "yes!"

YSBs Say

John, 43, Managing Partner, Consulting

I have been directly affected by the (expected) cultural bias that occurs when most of the leadership of the organization is of the majority race and I am the Black guy. It has driven me to over-deliver at every opportunity. It has driven me to focus on delivering business success, which usually trumps any biases.

Edward, 45, CEO, Supplemental Education Company

Race has helped my success, but in an atypical way. Coming from a lower socioeconomic level within the Black community, where very few people desired to excel professionally, made me "Super Ambitious." I think it was the economic component more than the racial factor. With my personality and background, I would have been just as ambitious if I was white and lower class.

Daniel, 38, Business Owner / Pastor

I feel that, being a Black man, there are many challenges that we face that could inhibit the pursuit of success. But to me, it really doesn't matter what race you are. What determines a person's success is the will and determination to look beyond the exterior and release one's inner potential to be everything that God created that person to be. I love being Black and everything about the essence of our culture and history. My race has aided me in every way and endeavor to pursue success. It is my job, as well as everyone else's, to seize the opportunity with every fiber of my being and never back down from any challenge that life has to offer.

Brian McClellan

"Racism is irrelevant"

Sometimes life is pretty "black and white." There are only two possible outcomes, winning and losing. Only one team wins the game, only one company gets the customer's business and only one guy gets the girl. Black and white. In none of those cases is there a prize awarded for mitigating circumstances. As Americans, we value results, not *"yeah, but…"* Results don't care about excuses, so should we? So often, life is simple. It is or it is not. One cannot be partially pregnant or partially faithful to one's spouse or partially honest. You are those things or you are not. It's just that simple.

In a results oriented world, no prize is awarded for the knowledge that one's path is more difficult than her neighbor's. Someone who graduates from Harvard Law School does not get extra credit for having to work to pay her way through school. The achievement and its benefits to the individual willing to make that sacrifice are worth the work. Often this person will value the experience even more and make even more of the opportunity because it was hard earned.

With that said, how are Blacks served by believing, or even knowing, that our path to greatness is harder than that of our neighbor? Will we get extra credit for this belief after we have "made it?" Can we fall just short of making it, but be given a pass because we are Black? Like Olympic diving, will our achievements in life get a boost for degree of difficulty? Of course, the answer to these questions is "no." Our YSBs know this, so many of them choose to view racism as irrelevant. They are all about winning and defeating any obstacle that stands in the path of winning. Race is simply one more obstacle that they will not allow to deter them from being successful. In life, there are no prizes for degree of difficulty, so we should not make any concessions for our difficulties. The YSBs choose to win, as should we all. It's just that simple.

YSBs Say

Shonika, 35, Pioneer of Youth & Teen Entrepreneur Coaching

Over time, I have grown to learn that the inhibitions I have had regarding race and gender have been my own. What I once thought were issues of race, I later realized were, more often than not, a lack of self-confidence and my inability to 'brand' myself personally or professionally. When you look at the most successful people, whether it is in business or a "social" environment, they have built a brand so that people want to compete to (partner) with them. (Conversely) the vast majority of people and companies think of building a brand as a way to effectively compete against others in the marketplace.

When people are trying to get their foot in the door, they often compromise themselves to "prove themselves." This is often based on their insecurities about their race, their gender, or their level of experience. Essentially, they have already substantially decreased their value and net worth. Everybody wants to know WIIFM (What's in it for me?) and why are you offering your services. If you come into the room with low self-worth and lack an objective or a mission, then it appears you have nothing to bring to the table. People don't want to "put all their goodies on the table" for fear you have nothing to give in return.

(Therefore), if you want to become a powerful person, you must empower others. Give people access to resources and people in your Rolodex and ask nothing in return. The greatest thing that can contribute to your success is to be trusted. You have to have self-confidence (as if) you've done this a million times and, therefore, everything is going to work out in a mutually beneficial way no matter what. Realize that sometimes you have to "fake it 'til you make it!"

Kevin, 33, Vice President, Banking

In some instances, I believe that race has provided me with opportunities to be considered for positions that traditionally would not have been available to minorities. I also believe that, in some instances, race has caused me to be overlooked for opportunities that could have provided a pathway to becoming more successful. However, I strongly believe that my success is purely based on God-given abilities that allow me to take advantage of the opportunities at hand.

Monica, 38, Owner, Public Relations Consulting Firm

The only role race has played in my successes, as well as my challenges, is that it has provided me with a unique perspective (on life). It has afforded me the opportunity to educate, celebrate, and influence and it has made me more determined to succeed, in spite of everything.

Twanna, 33, Writer / Blogger

An adult survivor of child abuse in Illinois and Mississippi, I didn't have an easy start in life. My parents were poor, and they divorced when I was young. At times I was raised by different relatives. It would be easy to be very bitter and angry about my early experiences. Instead, I've channeled that energy into building resilience against the things that life's thrown my way. Therapy. I swear by it. As for my career, I've certainly worked in spaces and with organizations where I was either the only person of color on the team or the only person of color in the department who wasn't a member of support staff. I wouldn't say that my race automatically aids or inhibits me.

Generally speaking, I surround myself with people—regardless of race/ethnicity—who support me. They're on my team, rooting for me. They pick me up when I fall, and they encourage me when I succeed. One of the best pieces of advice ever given to me (was this), "Don't automatically assume that everyone who doesn't look like you is against you, and don't assume that everyone who looks like you is for you."

"A double-edged sword, but one that made me stronger"

Experience is a great teacher to those who heed the lessons. Successful people see hard times today as simply a prelude to better times tomorrow. They very seldom regret even the most difficult of circumstances in their lives because those circumstances left them better prepared to seize future opportunity and to enjoy it. Successful people are positive people who are always studying the silver lining rather than the cloud. Those who do not succeed simply remember hard times as, well, hard times. Worse still, they may remember a failure as a reason not to try again. All people endure hard times, but successful people just view them differently.

Many of our YSBs share the lessons learned, or hard times, they have experienced as a result of being Black. Yet, to a person, they believe these hard times were a necessary component of their success story, if not the reason they have success stories at all. They insist upon learning a lesson from every experience in life so those experiences will not be wasted. They do not waste time lamenting the difficulties that come with being Black. They clearly articulate the good and the bad, but consider being Black net positive. These YSBs believe that being Black adds to, rather than detracts from, their success.

YSBs Say

Michele, 44, Fellow, State Government

Race has impacted my successes in both negative and positive ways. I have been given opportunity due to my race and my race has seemingly prevented me from getting opportunities I firmly believed I was qualified to fulfill. As an African-American female, I have been given an opportunity to participate at times simply because I satisfy two minority groups. While that fact may anger or annoy me, I try to use what may have been done just to satisfy a quota to my advantage. This behavior often inspires me also to succeed. It has been an opportunity to showcase my talents and abilities, prove the naysayers wrong, and shine.

Joyce, 39, High School Principal

Race has been a hindrance and a help. In some situations, people have assumed I was less qualified for a job/role due to my race (i.e., when on Back-to-School Night a parent asked me where I went to college when I taught at a diverse high school). In other situations, my race has been an asset. I was hired as the founding principal of a new, urban high school which replaced a low-performing school that is a community institution. The fact that I am comfortable with the community and the product of a similar community and they are comfortable with me was a plus. So, there are two sides to this coin of race.

Mark, 48, VP – Sales & Marketing, Media

Race, in my case, has potentially been a "double-edged" sword. To the positive, I know that I've benefited from affirmative action programs starting as far back as high school. Due to programs geared to inner city (read minority) youth I was able to get a scholarship to an elite prep school. Race has always given me a "different" status which set me apart from the crowd (good and bad) and gotten me noticed by the organization. Conversely, race has also helped set me apart from the "white guys" clique in some of the organizations of which I've been a part. Overall, to my knowledge (since I don't know what went on when I was out of the room), I would have to say that race has been a "net positive" for me given that the majority of organizations actually provided real opportunities for me to learn and grow.

Mildred, 40, University Assistant Professor

With my work as a writer, (race) has been of enormous value. It's allowed me to see the world from many different perspectives since as an African American one has to see the world from multiple Black perspectives—urban, rural, and from the majority perspective.

In the workplace, that perspective has been an asset and has increased my visibility in the mostly white environments in which I've worked. What has inhibited me is subtle but insidious. (I have been inhibited by) the constant presumption—or fear of the presumption—that we are inferior, the insults and disrespect which usually have to be absorbed as part of corporate survival. Although fellow people of color are rarely in a position to yield any real power over a career, the haters and blockers are of concern as well. That being said, the energy that goes into forcing yourself to stay open for unexpected allies and to watch for surprising foes is considerable. When I lived briefly in Kenya, I was amazed by how much removing racism as a day to day, direct reality, freed me up. We don't think about the one hundred compromises we make in a day to adjust to racism.

John, 38, Asst. Professor, Major – U.S. Army

Race has played an important role in my past and current success on and off the job. Often, organizations in the public, private, or non-profit sectors will claim they are looking for diverse candidates or people of color. No doubt affirmative action or organizations that desire to add diversity in order to reflect their clients' backgrounds has helped me and others get an interview, get recommended for a job or promotion, and in some cases get a special assignment or rotation.

On the other hand, being Black has created more scrutiny in my work, a set of additional eyes on my work quality, and the added pressures of representing my race or explaining my race. "Why do Black people sit together in the lunch room?" I can't answer this question. I often joke with my co-workers that when I am late or leave early everybody notices because I am Black. However, when someone white or female is out of the office, no one notices until the end of the day. I think all races have their challenges. However, being Black has the extreme on both ends. We just need to make sure our environment and experiences gives us more positive successes than failures.

Dwain, 48, Managing Director, Consulting

It has been a two-edged sword with huge benefits and some degree of reaching a ceiling. Race has contributed to the many job changes that I've made (nine in twenty-five years). For perspective, until making a career/industry change, each role offered higher levels of compensation. Race was a consideration in many of the hiring decisions companies made when adding me to the staff or leadership.

For my first post-MBA position from Atlanta University, the companies that recruited on campus were looking for talented African-American junior executives by definition. Thus, I was in a pool of diverse candidates for those entry level roles. Among several of the subsequent positions that I had, part of my appeal was the resume, the other was that I was also diverse. This proved to be a tie breaker on at least one SVP role versus a colleague that I knew happened to be a majority male and the other finalist in the selection process.

In most of my roles as a director or above, I was the most senior African American for at least one of the following: function, division, or company. Thus, when I was hired, I also enabled the organizations to demonstrate an open mind to diversity. On the flip side, race contributed to a number of mediocre reviews despite outstanding results. This was in part due to my own naïveté, and also to not fully understanding "the game."

One has to know "the game" to master it. It is also not a game you can simply study or read about in general, because the players in your world are unique and different from the examples others share. In this world, I had many instances where I simply did not fit in as well culturally despite my best efforts.

Snake Bitten

Do you know how many people die of a snake bite every year? None. No one ever dies of the snake bite. It is the venom that kills them. This message, the central message of the speech that helped African American motivational speaker Craig Valentine win the 1999 Toastmasters World Championship of Public Speaking, is very apropos for the Black community. The venom of racism will kill us if we allow it to stay in our bodies too long. Our ill will toward an individual racist, a group of racists, or a racist system rarely adversely impacts them, but it can rob us of our life force. Are we ready to die like this?

Of course, our race is something we cannot change, so how we choose to view our race is an important decision. Too often we choose to view being Black as being snake bitten, as some bad luck with which we have to deal. However, we and we alone choose how we view our race. There is no law that can be passed or apology made or reparations paid that can make us think differently. We must make a new choice ourselves. We can choose to look upon our crooked path to this place and this time as a positive. We can choose to accept our legacy as warriors whose spirit could not be extinguished. We could choose to view our legacy as one of indefatigable perseverance rather than unbelievable misfortune. We could choose to view our legacy as proof of our strengths rather than a reminder of our weaknesses. No one can help us think differently.

We must choose to love ourselves. We must remember that, although we have been snake bitten more than our share of times, being Black is not the snake bite. Successful people love who they are, warts and all. They celebrate themselves, their heritage, their triumphs, and even their tragedies with pride because all of these experiences contributed to the people they are today. To love ourselves means loving our journey as well. We Black people cannot benefit from dwelling on our challenges, but we can benefit from embracing the best of who we are. We must celebrate our heritage and triumphs and expel any venom still remaining in our bodies from the snake bites we have endured along the way. We can survive an infinite number of snake bites as long as we never hang on to the venom.

Not surprisingly, when asked whether race would inhibit their success in the future, our YSBs responded with a resounding "no." Many would not concede that race would even be a factor in their future success. Others believe that being Black will help them achieve success in the future. Some believe that race will be a factor, but will not present any obstacle that they will not conquer. Our YSBs have been bitten by racism in their lives and, to be sure, will be bitten again. Nevertheless, you will not find any venom in them.

"Race will not inhibit my success"

Dwight, 28, Business Owner, Financial Services

I don't plan to allow race to deter me from anything I plan to accomplish in the future. I don't expect anything to aid my future success, outside of my "it" factor. The "it" factor is the creative DNA we all have that makes us unique. I do understand racism is out there, but if I entertained and reacted as some expected, I wouldn't have accomplished one-third of my success.

Crystal, 45, Manager, Fortune 100 Consumer Goods Company

I don't dwell on this being an inhibitor anymore. I am at a point now in my career in which I digest much more thoroughly the landscape, ask lots of questions, and speak only when I have something meaningful to include or add. I have received many life lessons and mentoring from some industry leaders who have helped me gain this wisdom. The point I am strongly emphasizing here is that I value me and know the results I can deliver to any organization. I am confident, and I love that I am a Black woman with the credentials that I have. I control my own destiny.

Dwight, 46, Insurance Professional

I do not expect race to play a role in my future success. I have learned to go for what I want no matter what others say. If you do not go for it you will not get it. If you do go for it you increase your chances of success (dramatically). I believe success lies within the person.

Abdul, 24, Editor, Publishing

I try to never look at my race as inhibiting my success. While there is racism–and may always be—that should never shape how I view myself or what kind of work I put out there. If my grandparents managed to own a house and move to New York City and make it, there's very little excuse for me not to make it.

Shalom, 36, Author

My race will continue to influence me to excel. I refuse to let it be an excuse for failure.

Renea, 37, Graduate Student

I don't think race ever inhibits me. It might limit the way other people perceive me due to their own shortcomings, but it never inhibits my own expectations. Insofar as my race has aided me, I felt confident about grounding my understanding of the world in my African American heritage. That interest fueled my intellectual pursuits and my professional choices. Whether or not I work in positions that draw from that subject expertise in African American culture, I attribute my skills as a teacher, manager, writer, speaker, community servant, daughter, partner, and future parent to that grounding. I understand that part of what makes me unique and a valuable, productive contributor to society is my race, and my gender, and my individual experiences.

Antonia, 23, Newspaper Staff Writer

Minorities are not a dominant force in the media and many newspapers are looking to diversify their workforce. I believe that my talent, as well as my race, will be beneficial in future endeavors.

Natascha, 29, Career Coach

I expect my race to help aid my career by being a successful Black woman who is a youth career coach. My focus is on the children and youth of today. What I have found is I've been called into Black organizations and predominately Black and Hispanic schools in order to speak to the students about careers. I find that even in the predominately Caucasian schools I've been called in to add a special voice and show that population of students that success comes in all genders and all races. One of my Caucasian mentors said I'm hot right now meaning: young, Black, woman with an MBA. So I said, okay—I guess that's a compliment…

"Race may be a factor, but I will conquer"

Tim, 45, Principal, Consulting Firm

I MUST overcome race as a primary identity. I must develop a healthier self-perception and self-awareness that transcends my racial identity.

Torin, 39, Business Owner, Executive Search

I don't expect it to change much over time. The fact of the matter is that minorities are projected to become the majority in the years to come. This transfer in status will undoubtedly have an impact on how things get done (policy, promise, promotion). My feeling is that most will continue to seek out professionals that are capable of bringing creativity and delivering results. Will we still have those that practice the subtle shams, the deployment of roadblocks, etc.? Absolutely. But in the face of change, they will be forced to operate under more scrutiny as the awareness of the new majority will be on the scene, more alert and more than willing to blow the cover off that type of prohibitive behavior. I expect to continue getting that which I go after.

Nichelle, Writer / Blogger

I think I will get to a certain level of success where some people will wonder if I broke into a field because of my race. I guess it would be a bizzaro affirmative action where I am considered special because I do all these cool things AND I am Black. People seem to get a kick out of it. For some reason, the way some people call me "amazing" is a little bothersome. Is it totally inconceivable that someone like me could achieve success?

CHAPTER SIX
KEEPING IT REAL?

"A Black man voting Republican is like a chicken voting for Colonel Sanders." – J.C. Watts, Sr.

As a Black adult, I know full well that I am supposed to be "keeping it real." Unfortunately, I have no idea what "keeping it real" really means. Do you? I know we have all sorts of unwritten rules about what "real" Black people should be doing. One of the most recent additions to the list of actions Black people must take to stay "real" is supporting Barack Obama for president. African Americans supported Barack Obama in overwhelming numbers during the 2008 Democratic presidential primaries. By the end of the primary season, Obama was receiving more than 90 percent of the votes cast by African Americans. Nevertheless, there were many prominent African Americans who chose not to support Obama in his bid to be the first African American president of the United States.

African American leaders such as Congresswoman Maxine Waters of California and Congressman Charlie Rangel of New York, to name two, are among the African American Democratic Party stalwarts who backed Senator Hillary Clinton throughout the primary season. As a result, many Blacks are mighty displeased with Waters and Rangel right now. *"How dare they stand between us and history?"* say the critics of non-Obama-backing African Americans. Civil rights era legend and Congressman John Lewis of Georgia initially supported Senator Clinton before changing his allegiance to Senator Obama about a month after the primaries began. Despite Lewis' change of heart, Black Georgia-based political opponents of Lewis used his early backing of Clinton as a rallying cry to mount the first Democratic primary challenge to his House seat in sixteen years. Undoubtedly, Lewis will not be the last person who stands to face consequences for violating this latest "keeping it real" rule.

Even I have to admit, upon learning about Blacks who were publicly opposing Senator Obama my first reaction was less than enlightened. *"How dare they stand between us and history?"* This was my first thought too. Immediately I recalled the stories my parents told me about the civil rights movement. I recalled the stories of the courageous people who fought for rights that those of us born after the height of the movement often take for granted. I remember stories of white and Black protestors lining up together to enter a restaurant which did not serve Black people. The protesters lined up in order by skin tone from lightest to darkest to force the restaurant owners to determine who was "too Black" to be served. I recall the images I had seen, the old news footage of protestors being arrested, attacked with clubs, turned away by hoses, or chased by dogs. I remember hearing stories about white boys addressing Black men as "boy" with impunity because, according to the social customs of that place and time, white children held a superior social standing to Black adults.

Despite all of the progress that has been made between the 1960s and today, the pain of many Black people who lived in that era still remains. As they retell every tale, the pain is as fresh as if these events occurred yesterday rather than forty years ago. And yet people who actually lived through this, who faced down those hoses, who were chased by those dogs, who were beaten, and who were jailed were now choosing to withhold their support for the very ideal they fought to bring about? Barack Obama was practically plucked from "central casting" to be "The One," the first Black candidate with a legitimate shot to be the president, and these Black leaders were backing someone else? I, like so many of us, was incredulous! I thought, "Off with their heads!" Then, *Seinfeld* popped into my head.

What does Jerry Seinfeld have to do with any of this? Nothing. I am really referring to Michael Richards, the actor who played the role of Jerry Seinfeld's friend Cosmo Kramer on the hit NBC sitcom. Richards touched off a firestorm in late 2006 by directing an N-word-laden rant toward a Black audience member who heckled him at one of his shows. Prior to the advent of YouTube, this incident may not have made the news or, if it did, would have been buried on Page 16. However, in our YouTube world of today, we were able to see Richards launch into his racist tirade firsthand. As soon as we saw Richards come with "N-word this" and "N-word that," it was on! Immediately Richards became enveloped in a "fecal storm" and began trying everything he could to save his career.

Michael Richards' public relations offensive to control the damage included many public apologies, including an appearance on the David Letterman show, and the now seemingly obligatory trip to see the Reverends Al Sharpton and Jesse Jackson. This was the stop on the PR junket that angered me the most. I thought to myself, "Why does everyone who offends the Black community feel as if they can go to Reverend Jesse or Reverend Al for absolution?" I don't recall electing either reverend to represent me, but countless non-Blacks behave as if one or both are the "President of Black America." It is as if the Black community is a foreign nation with which the likes of Michael Richards and Don Imus negotiate through our appointed representatives. I found it more than just a little insulting that we again were being viewed as one large monolithic group.

The notion of seeking out the "President of White America," the one person who speaks for all white people, would undoubtedly seem ludicrous to them, so why are so many of them so willing to believe that the Black community has such a representative? Richards' move to seek forgiveness from Reverends Sharpton and Jackson to smooth things over with the Black community was his second wildly racist move in my mind, and one I took harder than the first. "How dare he assume that he can make his racist comments go away by simply satisfying Sharpton and Jackson? How dare he assume we all think alike?" Then my thoughts snapped back to Waters and Rangel. And I was busted.

I was outraged at Michael Richards for the same thought process that I was employing a little more than a year later. "Real" Black people think in one specific way. In reality, it is foolish to expect all Black people to take one and only one side of an issue. It is foolish no matter who holds the expectation. It's even worse when we Black people hold that expectation because we should know better. We know that we are not thirty-eight million people who share one brain. We should know better, so we should act like we know better. We cannot condemn Michael Richards or anyone else for assuming all Black people think alike when we demand the same uniformity from each other. We can't have it both ways. In fact, insisting upon having it both ways is preventing our success. We have to build a tolerance for diversity of thought within our own community so we can use that diversity of thought to better solve the challenges within our community. However, embracing this diversity would force us to redefine, or rather define, the phrase "keeping it real."

Finding the Double Agents

Where are all the "real" Black people anyway? Have you ever felt as if you were about to get your Black Card revoked? I know I'm not the only one. If your "realness" is at all in question, you'd better be careful. There is a band of Keeping It Real Police who will revoke your Black Card if you are not careful. However, if we truly excommunicated everyone who violated one of the unwritten "keeping it real" rules, there wouldn't be any "real" Black people left.

There was a time in our history when it was critically important to know which Black people were truly down with the cause and which might be double agents. For example, Harriet Tubman needed to know how to spot a double agent. Tubman, of course, was the conductor of the Underground Railroad, a remarkable operation in which she personally helped free more than seventy slaves from 1849 to 1860. The Underground Railroad was successful due to skillful planning, coordination, and an unwavering trust among its "engineers." An elaborate network of safe houses provided by white and Black abolitionists served as the "stops" on the railroad, and Negro spirituals were used to communicate coded messages all along the route. "Departures" were timed within the calendar year and even the day of the week to provide the best chance for the runaway slaves to elude capture. In an operation such as this, it was imperative that Harriet Tubman knew who she could trust and who would potentially sell out, thereby putting the operation and the lives of "passengers" and "engineers" at risk. Of course, at that time, being a member of the Underground Railroad was a capital offense. Therefore Black people then had to smoke out those who might sell out. They had to find the double agents.

More than one hundred years after the successes of the Underground Railroad, working for social justice was still extremely dangerous work. Just as it was dangerous to work on the "Railroad" one hundred years before, it was dangerous to be on the front lines of the civil rights movement in the 1960s. The forces that opposed the Underground Railroad were no less invested in the status quo during the 1960s and only slightly less violent in their approach to keeping it in place. The assassination of Dr. Martin Luther King will always be the highest profile example of the risk of working for social justice in the 1960s, but it was far from the only example.

In 1963, Medgar Evers was gunned down in his own driveway only months after becoming the NAACP's first field secretary in Mississippi. In June 1964, also in Mississippi, "Freedom Riders" James Chaney, Andrew Goodman, and Michael Schwerner disappeared and were found murdered two months later. The success of the civil right movement increased the threat to the status quo and therefore the mortal danger to those leading successful protests. These civil rights leaders could not afford to give ample advance warning regarding meetings or protest locations to those opposed to the cause because people commonly "went missing" during that time never to be seen again. Therefore, Black people then had to smoke out those who might sell out. They had to find the double agents.

Now let's fast forward to the 1990s. If you were to type "1990s sellout" into a Google search, one of the first search results would be about the rapper Hammer. In fact, Hammer appears prominently in the definition of the phrase "selling out" in Wikipedia. As you may recall, Hammer reached No. 1 on the Keeping It Real Police's Most Wanted List during the height of his popularity in the 1990s. According to many Black people back then, Hammer was a "double agent" who needed to be smoked out.

Let me ask you a question. Whose life did Hammer put in danger with *2 Legit 2 Quit?* What was his crime? There were too many non-Blacks buying his records? He was making too much money? He was more famous than hip-hop artists who had been in the game longer? In which of these "crimes" was Hammer in the wrong? By the 1990s, our double agent radar had clearly run amok.

The irony of the whole Hammer situation is that he lost everything because he was too supportive of Black people. Hammer was forced into bankruptcy in part because he had more Black people on his payroll than his income would support. More ironic still, when Hammer dropped the "MC" from his name and returned to the stage with a more "authentically Black" image, we didn't like that either. Remember Pumps and a Bump? We called that "fake." Again, what was Hammer's crime? His "crime" was being too successful, too good at what entertainers are supposed to do…sell records. More than a decade later, the "sellout" label still sticks to Hammer. Worse still, our misguided practice of seeking and exposing people who we dubiously label sellouts still persists as well.

Keeping It Real?

We are all, and I mean all, too willing to impeach each other for petty crimes against Black America. But at what cost? We clearly have no consensus regarding what "real Black" means or any reason to believe that such a definition would benefit in any way. All this "policing" does is divide us and make us less likely to work toward our common goals. Yet I guarantee that every one of us has appointed ourselves a deputy of the Keeping It Real Police at some point in our lives to make a citizen's arrest of one of our fellow brothers or sisters.

Why do we believe we can or should enforce a set of rules that we cannot define and no one has ever seen in print? Maybe that's the problem. No one has ever seen the rules in print. Just for fun, why don't we write down these unwritten rules as they are currently enforced in practice today? Maybe this is how they would read.

THE "KEEPING IT REAL" RULES

Disclaimer (the fine print): Below is a partial list of the Keeping It Real rules. Any violation of these rules will make the violator subject to the revocation of his or her Black Card. Those who do not hold a valid Black Card will be considered "sellouts" and will be subject to unlimited ridicule by valid Black Card holders. Modifications, typically additions, can be made to these rules at any time for any reason. Some of the rules herein are considered grounds for Black Card revocation by some valid Black Card holders but not by others. Some of the rules herein are considered grounds for Black Card revocation by valid Black Card holders some of the time, but not all of the time. Some of the rules herein are grounds for revocation in all cases except for the exceptions, which are made on a case-by-case basis as determined by an undetermined subset of valid Black Card holders.

THE FOLLOWING ARE GROUNDS FOR BLACK CARD REVOCATION

Being highly acclaimed by the mainstream media – Individuals who are highly acclaimed by the mainstream media can be subject to discipline up to and including revocation of his or her Black Card. In most cases, to become acceptable to the mainstream media, said successful Black Card holder will have had to adapt to mainstream sensibilities and therefore reject acceptable

Black Card holder behavior.

Examples of unacceptable means to garner mainstream success include using an overly sunny disposition to win over predominately non-Black audiences (see Al Roker, Wayne Brady, Bryant Gumbel) and making traditionally Black-only disciplines popular in the mainstream (see Hammer). Those seeking success in fields considered to be "white areas" (for example, hockey, auto racing, and country music) will also be subject to Black Card revocation. Receiving mainstream media acclaim is acceptable when said success achieved in acceptable "Black areas" ("Black sports," "Black music," comedy, and certain dramatic TV and movie roles). Those who garner mainstream success in "Black areas" will not be held personally responsible for the amount of acclaim they receive from the mainstream media (see Beyoncé). Exceptions will be made to the above rules in cases in which the valid Black Card holder demonstrates extreme virtuosity in "white areas" (see the Williams sisters).

Having success in a corporate environment – Achieving success in a corporate environment is generally frowned upon and can be grounds for Black Card revocation. By definition, to be successful in corporate America, said successful Black Card holder will have had to model the speech patterns, mannerisms, and fashion sense of the dominant culture and therefore reject acceptable Black Card holder behavior. However, large corporation success is acceptable if said successful Black Card holder demonstrates sufficient ambivalence toward his or her own success when among other valid Black Card holders.

Further, said successful Black Card holder must also take every opportunity to convey distaste for the corporate environment when in the company of other valid Black Card holders. Any overt joy or apparent comfort displayed with the corporate environment may be considered "acting white" (full definition below) and will leave the offending Black Card holder subject to discipline up to and including revocation of his or her Black Card.

Being a Republican – It is unacceptable for valid Black Card holders to be registered Republicans or to vote Republican except in extreme cases.

This is seen as a demonstration of the rejection of the political party that has brought Blacks unparalleled community-wide prosperity (with the exception of current crime rates, high school dropout rates, teenage pregnancy rates, etc.). For Black Card purposes, the definition of "Republican" will also include those who consistently embrace views generally held by Republicans (see Clarence Thomas, Condoleeza Rice). Republican Party membership and activism can be tolerated on a case-by-case basis as determined by an undetermined group of valid Black Card holders. A Black Republican can retain his or her Black Card if said Black Republican shows sufficient ambivalence toward being a Republican (see General Colin Powell).

Dating / Marrying Interracially – It is generally unacceptable for valid Black Card holders to date or marry non-Blacks, and such behavior is subject to discipline up to and including revocation of his or her Black Card. Dating interracially, until further notice, will not be seen as a positive demonstration of the "content of their character" ideal, which is the underpinning of the modern civil rights movement, but instead as a rejection of acceptable Black Card holder behavior subject to discipline up to and including Black Card revocation. Black Card holders who have chosen to marry interracially will be considered to have voluntarily relinquished their Black Cards except in the cases described below.

Dating or marrying interracially is always unacceptable for female Black Card holders, except in the case in which the valid Black Card holder is extremely attractive and otherwise accomplished in a "Black area" (see Halle Berry). However, the above rules never apply to male Black Card holders successful in "Black areas" as defined above. It is acceptable for the celebrity male Black Card holder to marry a non-Black female as long as she is extremely attractive. Further exceptions will be made in cases in which the non-Black spouse of valid Black card holder has been granted honorary Black Card status (see Former President Bill Clinton). Should an honorary Black Card holder marry a valid Black Card holder, said Black Card holder would not be subject to discipline.

Acting white – All of the prohibited behaviors described above will be collectively known as "acting white." As earlier described, violation of any of the above rules will be grounds for the revocation of the Black Card of the violator. In addition to the above, there are a number of other behaviors that are also categorized as acting white. Engaging in "white recreational activities" can also be considered "acting white" and leaves the actor subject to Black Card revocation. Some examples of "white recreational activities" are listening to "white music" (country, rock, country rock, grunge, so-called classical, etc.) and watching "white sports" (swimming, auto racing, tennis—except the Williams sisters, and golf—except Tiger Woods). A Black Card holder can also be deemed to be "acting white" for not expressing sufficiently vociferous interest in "Black areas" as defined above.

Additional examples of "acting white" include, but are not limited to, the excessive speaking of proper English among Black Card holders, excessive prioritization of academic pursuits to the exclusion of involvement in "Black areas," or being critical of the behavior of valid Black Card holders when among non-Card holders. The behaviors considered to be "acting white" can be changed for any reason and at any time by a holder of a valid Black Card.

The "Real" Problem

Here's the real problem with "real." We have not been very good historically about separating true "selling out" (a cowardly slave who dropped dime on Harriet Tubman) from jealously and envy (criticizing Hammer for being a successful entertainer). The "real" Blacks are unsuccessful and the successful Blacks are made to feel guilty about their success, a no-win situation for the Black community as a whole and everyone in it.

There was a time when the success of a Black person, any Black person, was a reason to rejoice for all Black people. Too often today, rather than rejoicing in the success of our brothers and sisters, we try to dream up reasons why that success is not "real." Too often, we condemn the most successful Blacks among us with the labels "race traitor" or "sellout" when their greatest offense is being good at what they choose to do. No doubt many Blacks who live this everyday are baffled by it, the words of LL Cool J's song *Illegal Search* ringing in their ears. *"Is it my job to make sure I'm poor?"* All of this begs another question. Why does so much of the peer pressure we place upon each other serve to promote our failure rather than our success?

This much is true. The speed with which we hurl insults like "sellout" at each other is inversely proportional to the speed at which we will succeed as a people. Translation: *Divided we fall.* Every day, we are getting less wealthy, less educated, and possessing of a weaker support system to change our circumstances. We all need to come together fast. We need Black Republicans and Black Democrats to join hands in brotherhood. We need corporate brothers and sisters to join hands with the entrepreneurs. We need the wealthy brothers and sisters to join hands with the less wealthy ones. We need to come together for a set of common causes about which we should all be passionate.

We cannot afford to chase fool's errands when we have real problems to solve. Why are almost half of our high school students dropping out of high school in an economy in which a high school diploma is not even the full price of entry? Why are more than half of our children born to unwed parents when we know that children born to unwed parents are born eighty yards behind in a one hundred yard race? Why do we steal from each other and commit violent crimes against each other at such an alarming rate? Why do we do it at all? Do we hate each other that much? These questions need to be at the center of any discussion we have as a Black community about what is "real."

To solve our real problems, we need to stop creating fictional ones. Which is more important, making sure we are dressed "correctly" or making sure our children can read this sentence? How long will we fixate on our people's choice of music or mate as a means to decide who is suitable to join our fight for our collective success? When the flood comes, everyone is supposed run to the riverbanks and start filling sand bags. In an emergency, every set of hands is a good set of hands if they are willing to work.

Friends, we are in the midst of an emergency. We have to be willing to bring together all of the incredibly talented, diverse people who call themselves "Black people" in the name of our common good. We have to be ready to work together rather than being content to drown as long as those standing on the river's edge with us are dating the "right" people or engaged in the "right" activities. Please tell me we know what time it is.

We cannot afford to be color-blinded and stay color-blinded. We cannot afford to confuse our real issues by trying to determine who is "really Black" based upon definitions that are misguided at best and suicidal at worst. It is not an exaggeration to say that we are in a war for survival today. We cannot afford to throw so many willing soldiers to the wayside. We do not have so many able bodies that we can afford to turn them away at the rate we currently do. We cannot afford to foster the level of dissension in our ranks we currently do with the charges of "sellout" and countercharges of "lazy (fill-in-the-blank)." We must end this civil war today and turn our muskets toward the real enemy before it is too late. Make no mistake about it. "Too late" may not be tomorrow, but it's the day after tomorrow. We can't wait another minute longer to get started.

CHAPTER SEVEN
THE NEW REAL

No question invoked more passionate responses from our YSBs surveyed than a question about "selling out." The question was posed as follows:

> *Some successful Blacks have been praised as "staying Black" or "keeping it real" while others have been condemned as "sellouts," "acting white," or even as "race traitors." Do you believe that there is a "right" way to succeed as an African-American? If so, how so? If not, why not?*

The passion stirred by this question was often mixed with pain and anger as if wounds from the recent past, or even the present, had been reopened. Almost every respondent had firsthand experience with being labeled a "sellout," many by someone who was supposed to love them. By reviewing the responses, you would think that being successful *equals* "selling out" to many Blacks, that there is no way to be successful and "stay real" at the same time. After studying these responses, I started to feel the pain.

Which other community considers its members disloyal simply for being successful? Isn't this what we are trying to do in life, have success? There is no greater violence we can do to each other than to discourage our own success. Judging by the YSBs surveyed, we often force each other to choose between loyalty to the Black community and success. We have created a situation that can feel hopeless, a no-win situation in which there are only two less than desirable options: failure and bittersweet success. We are robbing our own people of hope in a painfully similar way to how slave masters attempted to rob our slave ancestors of hope. It is disheartening to see that, in too many cases, we have continued the slave masters' work. This is what incenses YSBs in every corner of the Black community about the term "sellout." More than one hundred forty years after the Emancipation Proclamation, all Black people should be able to pursue success without the echoes of Willie Lynch ringing in our ears.

The Echoes of Willie Lynch

Willie Lynch was a slave owner in the West Indies in the early eighteenth century. According to legend, Lynch was summoned by Virginia slave owners to teach them how to control their slaves. The message that Lynch was said to have delivered was astoundingly counterintuitive upon first inspection. Reportedly, Lynch told Virginia slave owners that the key to controlling slaves was to get them to control themselves and therefore accept their servitude. What? Of course that wouldn't work, right? Of course a group of people who were all subject to the same mistreatment would band together against the agent of that mistreatment for their common good, right? According to Lynch, the answer was "not necessarily."

Willie Lynch was said to have told the Virginia slave owners that slaves would control themselves and accept their servitude if the slave owners continually highlighted the differences between them and pitted the different groups against one another. Creating this internal conflict in combination with making the slaves dependent on the slave owner would create an environment of self-loathing among the slaves that would be "self-refueling and self-generating." Said differently, if the slave owners could create divisions among the slaves, these divisions would ensure they stayed perpetually enslaved. More powerful than physical chains, the mental chains would have an impact that would last for years, or perhaps forever.

I was careful to use a word like "legend" when describing this story because today the account of the speech itself is widely believed to be a hoax. However, there is a reason the story of Willie Lynch is so often repeated and cited in literature and film. Regrettably, the central tenet of the message itself rings true. The United States of America itself was founded upon the same message credited to Willie Lynch, *"United we stand. Divided we fall."* It is telling that the differences Willie Lynch allegedly told the Virginia slave owners to accentuate were the cosmetic ones (old versus young, light-skinned versus dark-skinned, course-haired versus fine-haired) that often divide us still to this day. The message rings true because we have seen too many cases within the Black community in which we have focused on the trivial and lost sight of our true common purpose.

The speech itself may be a hoax. Perhaps Willie Lynch never gave a speech to slave owners. Perhaps there never was a Willie Lynch. However, the message itself is profound and timeless. To defeat any group of people, encourage them to fight among themselves rather than their common enemy. There is no question the Black community is guilty as charged on this score. We have ignored this message to our detriment for far too long and to continue to do so will put us in further peril.

United we stand. Divided we fall. We all feel that the Black community would benefit from being more united. This is one of the first issues we cite, if not the first issue, when we ask ourselves, "What is wrong with the Black community?" Yet we cannot get the "united" part right. Too often, we erroneously expect "united" to mean that we should have the same opinion on every important issue. To the contrary, the pressure we place upon each other to adopt similar viewpoints on our biggest challenges works to our detriment. However, it is imperative that we coalesce around a common purpose.

What if that common purpose was our love for each other, for the Black community? What if we believed, I mean truly believed, that we had a vested interest in each other's success? What if we really believed that a child who was still homeless in New Orleans due to Katrina nearly three years after the storm was our problem even though he or she is not our child? What if we truly believed the fact that high school-aged students in Detroit who are failing to graduate at the rate of 75 percent, SEVENTY-FIVE PERCENT, was our emergency even if we don't live in Detroit? What if we truly believed that the hopelessness and despair felt among the least fortunate Blacks diminished the lives of the most fortunate Blacks? This is how loved ones feel about each other. People who love each other feel they have a common interest that is a part of, rather than parallel to or counter to, their individual success. If we began to believe in such a love, our common purpose would quickly begin to come into focus.

If this love for each other were our common purpose, then the guiding principles of our future actions would be clear. Just as a loved one does for another loved one, we would view all of our actions through the lens of what is good for the Black community. What is clearly not good for the Black community is this ludicrous notion of "real." It presumes that some subset of us knows better than the rest what is good for the Black community. It is a level of individual arrogance that destroys rather than uplifts. This arrogance is a demonstration of self-hate rather than self-love. For the Black community to become a stronger people, our individual actions, all of those actions, must be a demonstration of our love of the Black community.

We can start to demonstrate our love for the Black community by showing love toward each of its members. We can show our love by evaluating our actions against their impact on the Black community. The test is simple. If our action does not make the Black community better, don't do it. Further, if the action taken by another Black person doesn't threaten the Black community, don't criticize it. No one can harm the Black community simply by listening to country music, marrying a white person, or even voting Republican.

Perhaps if we had more Black Republicans, we would enjoy the "swing vote" status and the corresponding political benefits that every other sliver of the electorate except us has enjoyed at some point in the last forty years. Because we don't "swing" from party to party, we have created a circumstance in which Democrats don't value our vote because they know they can't lose it, and Republicans don't value our vote because they know they can't win it. Without "swing value," we have diminished influence in the political process. This is just one of the many ways that demanding the uniformity of "realness" does us much more harm than good.

We can start loving each other by developing a bias toward taking a more global view with our thoughts and actions. We need to start distinguishing real threats from the fake ones and only reacting to the real ones. For example, our future success as a community is not threatened by the speaking of proper English, one of the practices condemned as "acting white," but our future is threatened by discouraging the practice. Proper English is the language of commerce in America and all over the world. How are we served by not being fluent in "the language that money speaks?"

We are not made stronger by discouraging our own people from success. We can start today by loving each other. We can start today by demonstrating through actions, not just words, that we are smarter than Willie Lynch.

The Race Bait – Why Is It So Tempting?

I'm sure there must be times when the fish knows the worm it covets is attached to a hook. I'm sure it knows that in biting the worm, it is likely to bite the hook as well. It knows that its next bite could be fatal, yet the fish is willing to take the risk. The fish is simply unable to wait to find another worm. The fish takes the bait…and so often that is the last bite it will ever take. Of course, no matter how tasty the worm, it will not have been worth it. No meal is worth dying for. This is true about so many temptations. So often the upside is short lived, or not realized at all, and the downside lasts forever.

Similarly, we often find the race bait just as tempting. We have seen this bait hundreds of times. The boss who speaks to us in condescending racist tones is the bait. The TV or radio commentator who has been reliably racially insensitive his entire career but is still able to incite us is the bait. The brother or sister of whose success we are envious is the bait too. We have all seen the bait so many times, but too often we take a bite anyway. We go off on that condescending boss to prove that "we don't take any mess," but also ensure that we will never be the boss holding doors open for the next wave of aspiring YSBs.

We're on the hook. We go on crusades to get racist talking heads fired, spending our precious time on an effort that, even if wildly successful, won't improve one Black child's life. We're on the hook. We call the successful Black person a sellout. We use the phrase "I know better than to have success *that* way" as the salve we rub on our bruised egos. We're on the hook again. Often, taking the bait feels good at first, but it never stays good.

Yes, the race bait is tempting, but it's as fatal to the success of Black people as the hook is to the fish. Have you noticed how rarely really successful Black people take the race bait? Oprah doesn't react to insensitive statements made by her media brethren no matter how outlandish. She simply goes about the business of making the world a better place and printing money doing it. Barack Obama very rarely gets caught up in the politics of race despite the numerous traps his political opponents have tried to set for him. This unflappable demeanor has obviously served him very well so far. Michael Jordan never railed against "racial insensitivity" of management like so many other stars in his position have done, but there was never any question that he was running things when he was with the Bulls. It's not a coincidence that these all-time African-American greats rarely if ever allow themselves to get race baited.

Yet too often we Black people just don't get it. Too often, we are displeased when Black people show composure in the face of racism and we show our displeasure by condemning them as being passive or weak. We turn around and call these composed, successful Black people "sellouts." Please don't get it twisted. You could easily argue Oprah, MJ, and Barack are the most powerful people in their fields today, the ones who can call the biggest shots. Please remember that making noise does not equal having power. Having power equals having power. Here is the difference. Noise makers are controlled by their environment, strictly reacting to what is presented to them. Shot callers are working to create an environment that works for them and others. They are actively blocking out all that does not serve the grand plan. They are focused on the prize, not the noise.

Oprah knows she does not make any more money, build any more schools, or save any more lives through her charitable works by jousting with "talking heads." Therefore, she doesn't do it. Barack Obama is seeking the power to effect history-making positive change, a power conferred upon the president of the United States by the will of the American people through their votes. Do you know how much positive change Obama could create for Black people by being the president? Obama does and he also knows he will not earn any more votes by chasing down every racist comment or situation, so he doesn't. This is not a coincidence, but a lesson we must heed. Successful Black people are too busy to "hate on" other Black people and too smart to allow themselves to be taken off course by the rest. They don't take the race bait.

The Race Bait – Why We Must Avoid It

Successful Black people, the ones who are able to avoid the race bait, all have one trait in common. They are self-confident enough to focus upon "doing right" rather than "being right." They are self-confident enough not to be defined by the small issues. They take the quickest route to enduring success by putting that success above instant gratification. They will suffer the condescending boss temporarily because they are planning to be the boss. In fact, they are taking detailed notes on what that boss is doing so they we will be sure to avoid making his mistakes. They become tomorrow's bosses, the ones who create opportunities for other Blacks. Successful Black people are self-confident enough not to "hate on" their successful Black peers but instead to try to enlist them as mentors or partners. Successful people are not threatened by other successful people. Successful people attract like-minded others and work with them to perpetuate their mutual success. They become the mentors to tomorrow's YSBs.

Conversely, weak-minded people need to be "right" in every argument. They are willing to die to win a battle that should have never been waged, one that puts the winning of the greater war at risk. They can't see the long view. They can't see the hook beneath the worm. The condescending boss hooks the weak-minded. So does the racist talking head. The weak-minded want to prove "they don't take no mess," but only prove they don't know a trap when they see one. Weak-minded people find it very hard to be successful.

We are not a weak-minded people, so we should not emulate them. We are a strong-minded people. The truest demonstration of our strength will be when we consistently refuse to fall for the head fake. The head fake, just like the bait, can only hurt us if we bite on it. Our strength will shine through, as I know it will, when we celebrate quiet strength as fervently as we do the louder kind.

I know that we are strong-minded enough to neutralize the Willie Lynch strategy once and for all. I know we are smarter than the fish that knows the worm is attached to a hook, but bites the worm anyway. One day soon, we will become too wise to ever take the bait because we will instantly spot the hook and recognize the danger therein. One day soon, we will no longer be tricked, even by our own people, into fighting each other. I know we regret destroying our own neighborhoods in protest of events in which we were treated unfairly due to our race. In retrospect, we understand how self-destructive that was. I know we regret looking at each other and seeing differences rather than diversity, adversaries rather than allies. In retrospect, we understand how self-destructive that was. I know we have seen the damage done by giving in to temptation, by reaching for the bait. We are stronger now, so I know we understand what we must do next and when we must do it.

Embracing Our Diversity

One of the central themes of the civil rights movement and the subsequent movements it spawned was the inalienable right of all people to be protected under American law despite their differences. Implied therein is that everyone has the right to be different and that diversity itself is valuable to any group or organization. We African Americans have argued that diversity is not only a moral imperative, but a business imperative. We have argued that diverse talent makes companies better by enabling the development of better solutions to customers' needs. We have argued that diverse communities increase the quality of life for all by bringing a variety of experiences in which we can all share. Businesses, cities, and countries have a competitive advantage when they create environments that attract diverse talents and allow those talents to prosper.

In fact, the diversity present in the United States is one of the reasons it rose to its current preeminent status on the world stage. America is a mighty nation in large part due to its historical ability to attract the brightest and most ambitious people in the world and its willingness to create an environment in which that ambition and intellect is rewarded. The diversity of its talent is America's most important competitive advantage. The Black community has been one of the most vocal champions of this diversity. Now we must practice what we preach. We must embrace the diversity within our own Black community as vociferously as we ask America to embrace us. We have no right to expect the latter if we will not do the former. More importantly, when we embrace our own diversity, we will gain the same benefits by welcoming those Black people we have historically shunned that we believe America would enjoy by welcoming us. We will build competitive strength rather than encouraging Black talent to "leave" the Black community. By embracing our diversity and therefore encouraging more diverse talent to stay "in house," we will be able to develop better solutions to the problems that plague us.

We must open our hearts to welcome love from all Black people, not just the ones who fit some stereotypical mold. We need to invite anyone who is willing to help Black people to be a part of the solution. We will need the talents of everyone who is sympathetic to the cause. To presume that any small group of individuals, the so-called "real Blacks," can know what is best for thirty-eight million people is a blinding display of hubris. Hubris like this destroys all it touches because it blinds its possessor to the facts. We cannot afford to be color-blinded any longer.

We shouldn't turn anyone away because we cannot predict from where our next world changer will come. I shudder to think what would have become of Tiger Woods had he been overexposed to the "Keeping It Real" rules as a child. If you know Tiger's story well, you know that he did not have a convention Black upbringing. You may know that Tiger's mother, Kutilda, is of Thai, Chinese, and Dutch descent and his father, Earl, is of African, Chinese, and Native American descent. To the consternation of many Blacks, Tiger does not even refer to himself as "African American," feeling that doing so would deny all the other parts of his heritage. The world may have defined Tiger Woods as Black, but he was never confined by an artificial definition of what Blacks were supposed to do or who they were supposed to be. As a result, Tiger was always free to pursue his love for golf rather than dismissing it as "something only white people did."

As it turns out, of course, Tiger had the talent and the drive to become arguably the greatest golfer of all time. This golf greatness has enabled him to become an agent for positive social change. His success has allowed him to found an eponymous school and charitable foundation that provides opportunities for minority children. His presence has forced the integration of dozens of golf clubs that were not integrated prior to his arrival to professional golf. Most importantly, he is changing minds and softening hard hearts about people of color and inspiring a generation of children of all races to dream.

What would have happened if we had discouraged Tiger from becoming Tiger? Had Tiger grown up in different circumstances, overexposed to the "Keeping It Real" rules, perhaps today he would be Eldrick Woods, anonymous member of society. The world would have been a lesser place if

Eldrick had not become Tiger. It is scary to think how many Tigers we have had in the Black community whose talent we never discovered because our narrow definition of "real Black" discouraged them from exploring those talents.

Opening our minds to a broader definition of "Black" can only increase our power, influence, and ability to have widespread success as a Black community. We need to encourage diversity among us so we are positioned to thrive in all environments. We need Black Republicans, Black Democrats, and Black Independents so we have a say in the political arena no matter which party is in power. We need successful Blacks in all industries so we can accumulate wealth in every economic cycle. We need to have successful Black people in all disciplines so the interests of Black people are represented at every table at which decisions are made. The more we encourage the members of our community to pursue success in the areas of their choosing, the stronger our community will become.

We in the Black community must build a culture that allows for another Tiger Woods, generations of Tigers. We must recognize that the child who is doing that unconventional thing for Black people could be the next world changer. He or she could be the one with the antidote sent here to cure us all. We must know better than to dissuade that child from greatness. We must love each other enough to open the doorway to success as wide as we can dream.

This is the message of our YSBs. They were incensed at the mention of the word "sellout" because they have felt its sting and seen the damage done. Yet our YSBs remain hopeful because they believe wholeheartedly in our ability to be great. They are living proof of our greatness. They know that if we embrace each other in all of our glory, our differences, and our similarities, we will start to command a power that is beyond description. Despite the mistreatment they have endured at the hands of Black people, they still love Black people and just can't help it. They have a love for the Black community, as so many of us do, that causes them to see us not only as we are but as we can be. I know you feel the same way. We will be astounded by what we are able to achieve when we abandon careless critiques of each other and begin to love each other as we should. Let's prepare to be astounded.

"Who you callin' a sellout"

The word "sellout," of course, is a fighting word to most Black people. It may be the biggest insult a Black person can hurl at another Black person. The damage caused by the indiscriminate use of this one word can last a lifetime. Calling someone a sellout means that person is a traitor, an enemy to Black values, anathema to all we hold dear. Therefore, the word "sellout" is the Black atomic bomb and should be reserved for use in only the most extreme of circumstances. Unfortunately, we have not been anywhere near that selective with its use.

Is there a right way, a "real Black" way, to succeed? This question got the attention of our YSBs, to say the least. The fact that we Black people toss the word "sellout" around so recklessly incensed our YSBs. They shared a great deal of passion and pain regarding their experiences with the notion of the sellout. In the strongest terms possible, they shared their advice about how we must change our attitudes regarding this word. I could go on, but our YSBs are itching to tell it like it is.

YSBs Say

Mark, 48, VP Sales & Marketing, Media

This is one of the most provocative issues that African-American business people face—and also one of the most patently absurd. First, there is no "right way" to succeed in the context of this question, as everyone's situation and upbringing is different. It is ridiculous to believe that a successful African-American Wall Street banker would be "successful" if he conducted himself in his "day job" like Flavor Flav, a successful African-American entertainer (to set up an extreme example). "Success" in any particular field can best be reduced to "knowing the best strategies to win," therefore there is no standard strategy into which African-Americans should be boxed.

(We have to look) beyond the superficialities of appearances (e.g. braces and a bowtie = sellout; Apple Bottoms and some Baby Phat = keeping it real) and answer the issue of how the individual views his or her membership and allegiance to the African–American community. To me, a sellout is someone—"successful" or not—who is working in some capacity against folks of similar heritage. If you are the most "successful" drug dealer on your block, I consider you a sellout—you are selling out your own folks for money, prestige, whatever. I would say the same thing about the Wall Street brother who, once inside the institution, works to make sure that he keeps the rest of y'all out. The fact that he bought his suits at Brooks Brothers is totally irrelevant to his "stayin' Black" score.

Generally, we can't claim to "know" most of the people we encounter in the street. Yet, in a flash, we are ready to make pronouncements about their "realness" or "sellout" quotient based on how they're dressed and who they may be with at that particular moment. I may be in my "interview suit" today because I'm trying to get a job and spend the rest of my time in FUBU at the community center working with "at risk" kids. Am I "acting white?" Since you don't pay my bills or take care of my kids, you don't know what I need to do to "keep it real" And what is the actual definition of "acting white" anyway? Not speaking ebonics? Wearing tailored suits and ties? Living outside of downtown? Having an advanced degree? Preferring something other than hip hop? And who are the arbiters that make that call?

I am always amazed that we spend so much time debating this rather immature point. This is the high school clique conversation writ large. We should spend a little more time understanding how ALL of us can work together to drive forward progress for ALL African-Americans, rather than find yet more reasons to keep us apart.

Mildred, 40, University Asst. Professor

(Right way to succeed?) Of course not. This attitude boxes people in and to no good effect. The weak-minded can be attached to values that don't fit them or their environment. What does it mean to "keep it real?" Loyalty to the less fortunate? How does that manifest? Language? Dress? Actions? Service? There is no real Black experience, though the media and even we have often characterized this as the experience of poverty or the urban experience. Sometimes "acting white" is a way of saying that successful strategies—studying hard, academic excellence—are the province of white people. Did they invent these things?

This is a disaster not just for African-Americans but for all those who lack privilege. I happen to believe that we should be about uplifting the race. Even if we wished otherwise, residential segregation often dictates a shared destiny. This can't be an excuse for other Blacks to be held up to scrutiny and for contempt. If people want to help, cool. If not, let's move on.

Edward, 45, CEO, Supplemental Education Company

Many paradigms in the Black community are myopic or narrow-minded. There is no one way to be Black, just as there is no one way to worship a higher power. During the pre-civil rights movement, we had an identified "common enemy." Although many whites from Quakers to staunch Liberals have fought and died for civil and human rights, our past common enemy had a white face and paradigm supporting white supremacy. Since Blacks no longer have a common enemy, factions within the Black community have opted to spearhead our direction. This wouldn't be problematic if we weren't so dogmatic in believing our way is the only way. Integration broke down racial barriers but created intra-racial barriers within the same race of people fighting for freedom. Our new enemy is ourselves.

Candace, 32, Public School Teacher

NO, I do not believe there is a right way or wrong way to act in order to succeed as a Black person. I, too, have been told I "acted white" or that I am a "sellout." I married a wonderful man who just happens to be white and we are expecting our first child this spring. We receive dirty looks in public, mostly from Blacks, but we have decided to ignore other people's ignorance. Some have even muttered slurs when they see us. All my life, I have attended schools that were predominately white, which allowed me to feel comfortable around white people. Never once have I felt out of place anywhere I have gone. Never have I felt uncomfortable going into any type of neighborhood. It is Blacks, however, who have judged me because I live a different lifestyle. I do not deny my Blackness; in fact, I am very proud of it. But to many Blacks, I am not "Black enough." Yes, I am mixed but that is not my fault nor is it something of which I am ashamed. Instead of putting people down, fellow Blacks need to be celebrating the diversity within our own communities.

Anonymous, 27

I remember watching an episode of Oprah, and her guests were Bernie Mac and Charles Barkley. They were all reflecting on distinct instances in their lives when they were referred to as a "sellout" or an "Oreo." They all laughed amongst each other at the painful accusations. As I watched them, I had my own "aha" moment of sorts. Growing up, I definitely experienced similar name calling from my African American classmates as I worked to achieve my goals in student government, music, journalism, etc. Those words were extremely hurtful and at times I found myself having to play down my aspirations and accomplishments just to fit in and be accepted.

I remember being a member of a Black social organization and the separation between the kids who lived closer to the big city and the kids who lived deep in the suburbs. It was uncomfortable and I would dread going because, despite the organization's well-intentioned purpose, there was a clear separation between those who were "Black enough" and those who were "too white." Thank God I made it through those times and entered the workforce where Blacks who spoke articulately were celebrated and hired faster than those who had previously teased me for being a "race traitor."

The irony in all of this is that all of us who were teased for "acting white" are now extremely active in majority African-American organizations and one of them is running for president! If we got caught up in the "right way" to succeed as an African-American, no one would ever succeed. We need to stay focused with our eyes on the prize and tell our children not to fret because things will get better for them after grade school. There is nothing wrong with being smart and ambitious. No one should be ashamed, but unfortunately many people feel that way. The African-Americans who were not "keeping it real" are now globally running top companies and graduating from Ivy League universities around the nation.

Marvin, 38, President, Consumer Goods Company

These phrases (like "race traitor") divide our culture even further. Every Black person has his or her own ideals and value system. What works for one Black individual does not always work for the next. In many instances, when a Black person adapts to the business environment that he is in he is considered a "sellout." Further, learning the "rules to the game" and using those rules to their advantage is in some ways seen as being a "race traitor" or not "keeping it real." How ridiculous! I don't believe there is a "right" way to succeed.

Michele, 44, Fellow, State Government

We are all unique individuals with varying experiences who respond differently as a result, therefore, I don't believe that there is any "right" way to succeed. What is "being Black?" How does one define such a notion? I do believe that feeding stereotypes for the sake of conforming to someone else's belief is ridiculous. Although criticized harshly by many within the Black community, I have to agree with Bill Cosby's assessment of how we articulate ourselves. As the daughter of an English teacher, I was taught and continue to speak in a grammatically correct fashion. Although I was often ridiculed by my peers as a child as "sounding white," whatever that means, as an adult I'm viewed primarily with great respect and seen as an educated professional.

I believe we do our children a disservice when we fail to act any way other than as respectable individuals. Children are like sponges, constantly observing and copying our actions more so than the commands placed upon them.

"To thyself be true"

Another sentiment that was prevalent among our YSBs is that Blacks too often follow a misguided notion of accountability. We expect each other to be accountable to a nebulous definition of racial authenticity, "realness," and an undefined tribunal of arbiters of said "realness." However, our standard of accountability when evaluating our own behavior is decidedly less stringent. Maybe this is simply human nature, our natural tendency to expect others to "do as I say, not as I do."

The YSBs have a different take. Many feel the best way they can honor the Black community is to model the highest standards of behavior. They aspire to be role model parents, spouses, children, citizens, and achievers. They believe if they behave in a manner of which their immediate family can always be proud, then the Black community should share that pride. According to our YSBs, those that do not respect such an approach must check themselves.

Oscar, 37, Business Owner, Entertainment Industry Consultant

There is one litmus test for success. If it lifts up others, your success is ordained. Otherwise, it is not. My first duty is to God…to the truth…to the good. Anyone (Black or otherwise) who is hurt by my doing right deserves my condolences (yes, doing right might hurt righteous people at times) or consternation (maybe those "hurt" are not "in the right"). Either way, I cannot see my moves as traitorous because I submit to the litmus test.

Dwain, 48, Managing Director, Consulting

I think that one has to be true to oneself. However, it is incumbent upon those in leadership roles to provide coaching to others. This doesn't need to be in the form of a 1x1 every other week. However, there are lessons learned at each level. If those learnings are not shared, the subsequent leaders risk experiencing unnecessary setbacks. By contrast, if they better understand the landscape, they can focus on their strengths and achieve greater success faster. This should be our goal, to expand the number of successful African Americans. This is a function of helping others. For those who have reached a position of leadership and fail to help others….they are failures. Their legacy is small and weak versus those who help others and build a strong group of leaders behind them.

Renea, 37, Graduate Student

No, there is no "authentic" way to be Black. Wonderfully, there are as many ways to be and see Black as there are people connected to "Blackness" as a social, political, and cultural expression. Unfortunately, in the smallness of our own experience we sometimes put limits on what we and others can be based on the boundaries of our own experience. People of African descent in the United States do have a connection to a unique historical, social, and political legacy. Part of that legacy is a sense of individual connectivity and collective responsibility. We are sensitive and vigilant about these points because they have provided a measure of protection to our community in times of crisis and an opportunity for advancement when there were not enough available in a prejudiced society. In the midst of struggle, however, sometimes people confuse what we are with what we are experiencing. Blackness is not poverty, strife, scarcity, struggle, or hard times. Those are challenges that we have had to face.

Twanna, 33, Writer / Blogger

The only "right" way to succeed as an African-American living in America—or in whichever country you may choose to reside—is to succeed in your own way. I've never been a fan of the "keeping it real" vs. "acting white" stuff because it's based on the premise that all Black people dress and talk exactly alike. It also assumes that all Black people like the same things. Frankly, that's BS. If we subscribe to the notion that it's not okay to pursue individual passions—even when those interests don't match stereotypes of what it means to be Black—we'll only shortchange ourselves and limit our own capacity to succeed. There are enough obstacles in life, don't add additional unnecessary ones with self-sabotage. A mentor once told me, don't let you—or others' notions of what's the correct or proper way to be you—stand in the way of your success.

Brian, 39, President, Financial Services

I believe you must remain true to yourself, your family, and community. Now that we have better opportunities to participate in the freedoms offered by our country, earned by previous generations, we must not abuse those sacrifices by disavowing ourselves of their sacrifices and struggles. While I do endorse being completely cognizant of the past, we cannot allow our past history and allegiances to prevent us from moving forward. My generation will likely be one of the last generations to have personal contact with those who marched with Dr. King and recognize firsthand the benefits of the civil rights movement. However, many African-American elementary and some high school students don't know the full extent of their legacy in America. That's tragic. As we [African-Americans] continue down the path of realizing the greatness and opportunity that America offers, we must be even more aware of the shoulders upon which we stand.

CHAPTER EIGHT
CAN'T WE DO BETTER?

To many Blacks, Bill Cosby broke the cardinal rule. In 2004, at the NAACP fiftieth anniversary celebration of the Supreme Court's decision in the Brown v. Board of Education case, Cosby put the Black community "on blast" with his now famous "pound cake" speech. In this speech, he went into great detail about the failings of the Black community. Cosby was fiercely critical of Black parents for abdicating our responsibility to our children. He argued that Black parents have created a generation of children that does not value the quality education that Brown v. Board of education helped make possible. He called us out for being missing in action while our children commit crimes but quickly decry police violence against our children when they are injured or killed while committing that crime, like Cosby's now famous example of the child "shot in the back of the head over a piece of pound cake."

Cosby gave us a heavy dose of tough love that the assembled crowd received very positively. I suspect that in our heart of hearts, the vast majority of us know that Dr. Cosby is right. Most of us agree that we are underachieving as a community and in some cases alarmingly so. Many of us agree that we all bear some responsibility for this underachievement. We all own a piece of our failures, either through our actions or through our inaction. Yet to many Blacks, Cosby crossed the line and, as a result, became a target for many Blacks seeking to revoke his Black Card.

The "pound cake speech" marked the beginning of a new act in Cosby's career in which he has transitioned from entertainer to activist. His 2007 book co-authored with Dr. Alvin Poussaint, *Come On People,* was a significant departure from his *The Cosby Show* persona and his popular 1987 comedy book entitled Fatherhood. In *Come On People,* as in his traveling speaking tour, he implores Black people to take responsibility for their lives and to live to a higher standard. When delivered live, Cosby's message is rarely met with anything but nods, if not shouts, of approval from the Black crowds with which Cosby speaks. Yet to many Blacks, Cosby is out of line. Why? Cosby's critics argue he has broken the cardinal rule by calling us out in the presence and full view of non-Blacks. They say Cosby was not sensitive enough of the challenges underlying our failures. This insensitivity, critics argue, was irresponsible because his message could cause more harm than good by giving Black community opponents ammunition with which to attack us. In the process, he exposed the new fault line within the Black community, the growing chasm between two camps of thoughtful Black people about what constitutes responsible Black behavior.

These two camps are getting dangerously entrenched in their respective positions. In one camp stand Black people who argue that our current circumstances are deeply rooted in the centuries of mistreatment we have endured in America. They are not against promoting personal responsibility, but they do not want to allow mainstream society "off the hook" either. This camp argues that we are not solely responsible, and perhaps not even primarily responsible, for our current circumstances. They feel that too much talk of personal responsibility not balanced by the role of those other parties responsible for creating Black community problems will, in fact, let those other responsible parties "off the hook." Such imbalanced conversation will give the federal and local governments, for example, license to abdicate their responsibility to help clean up the mess they help create within the Black community. Therefore, such conversation is seen by this camp as irresponsible.

The other camp on the other side of the fault line, the Cosby camp, sees the issue very differently. This group sees a Black community that is reversing the progress made by prior generations and accelerating the spread of new problems through our own bad behavior. They do not want to ignore history's role in our current circumstance, but they feel that the Black community is standing on a burning platform upon which we are pouring kerosene with our poor choices. Not speaking openly about these issues has exacerbated an emergency situation to the point at which we can no longer afford to address it quietly. To fail to sound the alarm is irresponsible, according to this camp.

As much as I disagree with "requiring" uniformity of though within the Black community, this is the one case in which we must choose a camp to support. We must come to a consensus on the nature of our problems, at the very least, before we have any hope of solving them. The vast majority of us would argue there are many things the Black community needs to change dramatically and quickly. However, there is a significant gap between the belief that our largest issues are ours to solve and the notion we require outside intervention to solve them. Each notion implies a complete different understanding of the issue and, therefore, a fundamental disagreement on the starting point. Even if we could agree on the destination, determining the correct route is impossible if we cannot agree upon where we currently sit.

The issues we face as a Black community are daunting, but equally threatening to our future in our inability to come together on a starting point from which to confront them. Until we can come to a consensus on the nature of the problems we are trying to solve, we need to keep talking and allow our love for the future of the Black community to trump any worries about who hears the discussion.

The Weight of Our Expectations

The largest sticking point between our two warring camps is the question of expectations. What level of behavior and achievement should we expect from each other in the Black community? A very interesting study about expectations was released in 2005 by Professor David Figlio of the University of Florida. This study concluded that students with "unconventional names," names with unusual spellings or punctuation, receive lower grades in school than siblings with more conventionally spelled names. Professor Figlio argues in his work, published by the National Bureau of Economic Research, that teachers and administrators subconsciously expect less from "DreQuan" than they do from "John," even when DreQuan and John are in the same family. These expectations manifest in a number of ways, including the attention a student receives in class, how the students' work is graded, and whether that student is selected for "gifted" programs in school. The implications of this study are many, but the key takeaway is this. Expectations matter. Expectations can drive outcomes. Which begs a very important question, *"Do we expect enough from each other in the Black community?"*

We have a number of issues within the Black community that threaten to negatively impact us for generations to come. Who is responsible for these problems? Too many of our children are being born out of wedlock. Moral issues aside, a child born without two parents in his or her home starts at a disadvantage that is extremely difficult to overcome. This child will miss the guidance and the stability that a two-parent household can provide. Children without this stability are more likely to drop out of high school, more likely to commit a crime for which they are incarcerated, and more likely to abuse drugs and alcohol. This child may feel this lack of guidance and stability for the rest of her life. This child is more likely to fail. Who should we, the Black community, blame for the rate at which Black children are placed at this disadvantage?

We have too many high school-aged children failing to graduate high school. In today's economy, the median non-high school graduate makes

$21,400 per year, the median high school graduate makes $30,200, and the median college graduate makes $49,350. Non-high school graduates are also three times as likely to be unemployed as college graduates, so there is no guarantee the non-high school graduate will make that median salary of $21,400. The United States Department of Health and Human Service Poverty Guideline (the "poverty line") is $21,200 per year in income for a family of four.

Failing to finish high school is tantamount to "signing up" for a life of poverty, which has far-reaching implications including lack of access to quality health care and quality legal advice. Poor people have less access to health care because they are less likely to have jobs that provide health care insurance. Therefore, poor people are more likely to get sick and stay sick. Poor people have less access to high quality legal representation as well. Therefore, if a poor person happens to get in trouble with the law, that person is more likely to serve time. Who should we blame for the rate at which Black children are undereducated?

We have too many Black people committing crimes. Unconscionably too often, the crimes Black people commit are against other Black people. According to the Bureau of Justice Statistics (BJS), as of 2001, a staggering 16.6 percent of Black men had entered a federal or state prison at some point in their lives. At current incarceration rates, the BJS estimates that 32 percent of all Black males alive today, nearly one in three, will spend some time in prison. The violent crime statistics are even more troubling. From the years 1973-2005, almost half of all murder victims in the United States were African American despite being only 12 percent of the population. Even more troubling was the fact that 94 percent of these African American murder victims were murdered by African Americans. It is impossible to calculate the impact that being a victim of a violent crime has on the psyche of the victim. This violent crime victim, if he or she survives the crime, often suffers emotional trauma that makes him or her more likely to perpetuate the cycle of misery by committing crimes in turn. Who should we blame for the rate at which we commit violent crimes, especially Black on Black violent crime?

It may be that the legacy of slavery and Jim Crow are primarily to blame for the circumstances in which we find ourselves. There is no question the wealth that many non-Black families enjoy today was built over the generations of opportunity they enjoyed, opportunity legally and systematically denied to Blacks for most of our history in America. Even those non-Blacks who were not born into wealth were less likely to have been born onto a "burning platform" as were so many Blacks. However, when we hold someone else responsible for a situation, the human tendency is to wait for the offending party to make the situation right. But is it responsible for the Black community to wait for someone else to cure what ails us? Even if we have a legitimate claim, can we afford to wait for them to come around to our way of thinking?

Remember the power of expectations. If we expect outside help to solve an issue, can we simultaneously take enough responsibility for that issue to solve it ourselves? A common saying within the Black community is *"You can make money or excuses, but not both."* Can we ever make our success while we are still trying to explain why we don't have it? Even if someone else is to blame, can we ever win while we steadfastly maintain a grip on our grievances?

Can't We Do Better?

I cannot accept the notion that my fate was determined fifty, one hundred fifty, or four hundred years ago. Perhaps it is my ego, as I have never been accused of lacking confidence, but I believe that I control my own fate. I believe that I can unrig rigged games through the force of my will, through learning how the game is played, and then outplaying the competition. I believe that I can outsmart or outwork anyone who would actively oppose my pursuit of success. I believe this because I have seen so many people who look like me do the same thing.

I believe that I am descended from a special group of people, a people who fought to live through systemized torture, a people who fought to learn despite being prohibited to learn, and a people who fought to love despite being surrounded by hate. The Black community has taught me that, as a descendant of a people this accomplished, I should recognize that my ability to achieve is unlimited. Therefore, I do not want to be graded against a diminished standard, patronized, or treated as anything less than the formidable force that I am. I am ready for the "big leagues" and have no use for a minor league standard. I am no different than you. I am you.

We all are descended from a special people. We are too gifted, too talented, and have too much potential in every discipline and in every way success is measured to accept a lower standard. We do not need patronization and should resent even the mere suggestion. We don't need a handout because we can give each other a hand up. Therefore, situations in which we self-sabotage drive me insane! There is nothing that represents our maddening proclivity toward self-sabotage more than the so-called "Stop Snitching movement."

The "Stop Snitching movement" is a push among some members of the Black community to promote the idea that there is absolutely no acceptable reason for Black people to cooperate with police. According to "Stop Snitching" advocates, no matter the severity of the crime or the innocence of the victim, it is a greater crime against the Black community to help the police apprehend the crime's perpetrator if that person is Black. As you can imagine, the biggest advocates of this "movement" are criminal-minded Blacks who want to commit crimes with impunity, mostly against other Blacks. "Stop snitching" proponents use our learned distrust of the police to keep us in fear of both them and the police. The astounding and frightening part of this movement is not that it exists but how effective it has been.

Just like any other product sold to the masses, the "Stop Snitching" initiative has even recruited high-prolife pitchmen, professional athletes, and rappers who, through their own ignorance or misplaced allegiance to the criminal-minded, advocate for this position. These pitchmen have sold their "product" well. On a story which aired on *60 Minutes* in April 2007, the news program interviewed Black teens who were startlingly unflinching in their support for allowing violent criminals to go free rather than helping the police to catch them. The scariest part of "Stop Snitching" is the fact that, unlike drug abuse or even the violent crime it protects which is universally recognized as "wrong," refusing to help the police catch Black murderers, even when they have murdered other Black people, is seen as "responsible" behavior.

All of this has me beside myself. Can't we do better? We call the assumption that all Black people behave the same way as the worst of us "racism." How should we categorize the assumption that all police officers behave the same way as the worst of them? We all know there are bad police officers. However, we have to admit that there are bad Black people as well. Any Black person who harms another Black person should not be worthy of our defense. Or do we hate police more than we love our own lives, our own futures? Are we willing to hand over our neighborhoods to criminals, throw away our futures, and teach our children to do the same simply out of spite? That is no smarter than burning down your own neighborhood in protest. If the people you are protesting don't care about you, doesn't destroying your own property give them more of what they want? We can and must do better. It's time to focus on what we want for ourselves. Do we want more crime or less? Do we want more education or less? Do we want more teenage pregnancy or less? Do we want more poverty or less? We are good enough to solve our own problems. We have a long history of rising up, so we need not lie down now. We do not need to shrink from this challenge. We can win. Not only can we win, but we should expect to win because we have won in dire circumstances in the past.

Again, we need to step into our power and accept the responsibility of that power. No one will ever be more passionate about solving our problems than we will. Therefore we will never get a better response to our problems than our own. We cannot afford to wait for someone else to fix this for us. And if getting outside help means convincing someone outside the community to take the blame for our issues rather than addressing them ourselves, we can't afford to lay blame either. It's just irresponsible.

CHAPTER NINE
RESPONSIBLY BLACK

Always do the right thing. This was the advice given by the Ossie Davis character, "Da Mayor," to Spike Lee's character, "Mookie" in the movie *Do the Right Thing.* This is easier said than done, of course. As the old saying goes, *"The road to hell is paved with good intentions."* Assuming we want to "do right" as a Black community, how do we know right when we see it? What is responsible Black behavior? Our YSBs again were profound and powerfully insightful in their responses.

Speaking Out is Responsible

Bill Cosby has been labeled as irresponsible by some Blacks for his approach in addressing the issues of the Black community for the last several years. However, we all know in our hearts that he was right. The Black community has been irresponsible, both in our actions and in our less than aggressive response to those actions. Again, we find ourselves in a situation in which we want to sit on both sides of the fence. We decry the "blue wall of silence" that seems to protect too many police officers accused of improper behavior within our communities. We rightly argue that police officers, sworn officers of the law, should pursue bringing the criminals within their ranks to justice every bit as aggressively as they pursue criminals on the streets. Given that this is our position on police silence, we cannot in good conscience remain silent when we have our own problems to solve. The only responsible approach to solving our issues within the Black community is to openly discuss them with each other without regard for who hears the discussion. Our silence no longer serves us. In fact, our silence in some cases is killing us faster than we realize.

A perfect example of the fatal nature of our silence is our response to the HIV epidemic—yes, epidemic—among Blacks in America today. While most Americans, African Americans included, appear to view HIV/AIDS as an African problem, a full-blown AIDS epidemic is occurring among African Americans right here at home. According to the Henry Kaiser Family Foundation, 50 percent of the new HIV cases reported in 2005 were reported by African Americans despite being only 13 percent of the population. More startling still is that half a million Blacks are living with the HIV virus today. This represents 2 percent of our population, which is the highest rate of infection among any rate of any ethnic group in America. In our nation's capital of Washington, D.C., an unbelievable one in five citizens is infected with HIV. The population of the District of Columbia, of course, is predominantly Black, 55 percent Black to be exact. In a five-city study performed by the Centers for Disease Control (CDC), the rate of Black homosexual males carrying HIV was a mind-bending 46 percent, a rate that mirrors the rates in sub-Saharan Africa about which we Americans are so alarmed.

Brothers and sisters, HIV in America among Blacks is an emergency, an epidemic. According to the CDC, a Black male is now eight times more likely to contract HIV than a white male, and a Black female is twenty-one times more likely to contract the virus than a white female. There are many reasons that have been offered by medical scientists, social scientists, and political scientists for the incredibly high infection rate among Blacks. Some cite the relatively short distance in social terms between high-risk and low-risk groups within the Black community. Said differently, those who demonstrate high-risk behaviors in terms of contracting HIV and those exhibiting low-risk behaviors are more likely to come in contact with each other in the Black community than within other ethnic groups.

Nevertheless, the HIV epidemic is not only in Africa, yet I was surprised to learn this about the extent of this problem among Blacks in America. Were you? Perhaps the better question is, "Why aren't we talking about this?" The response to this problem by the Black community has been no response at all. Are we so afraid of discussing our issues in "mixed company" that we are willing to die to stay silent?

It is irresponsible of us to try to keep our problems hidden so we can save face or maintain some "leverage" against the mainstream community by playing on their liberal guilt. Our problems are killing us, literally and figuratively. The only responsible response is to shout them from the rooftops so everyone in the Black community will hear them. Then we must enlist everyone willing to help into our "army" without consideration for what we used to call differences.

In a YouTube-cell phone-camera world in which everyone is potentially an "i-reporter," there is no practical way to have a private conversation that only Blacks would hear. Maintaining this "code of silence" would require that we not speak to each other at all. Whatever damage may be caused by opponents of the Black community hearing our issues would be far outweighed by the benefits of sharing the information about and the responsibility for solving those issues with as many sympathetic ears as possible.

In 2008, being responsible and Black means realizing that no one is "on the hook" for our problems but us. We cannot be concerned with how the open discussion of our problems, including our role in creating them and solving them, is received by a mainstream audience. We have to be more concerned with "doing right" than "being right." Again, we have to yield to love, in this case loving our future more than we fear those unsympathetic to our plight.

To what extent do you tailor your behavior personally, politically, or professionally out of a sense of responsibility to the larger Black community?

Love is Responsible

There was a decidedly different tone in the responses to the question above than the earlier "sellout" question. Family members can infuriate and frustrate us, but we can't help but love them because to love family is in a human's nature. Similarly, the Black community can infuriate and frustrate us, as was evident in the "sellout" question, but we still can't help but love it. In the responses to this question, the love these YSBs, and most YSBs, have for the Black community was on full display. Our YSBs have clearly put a great deal of thought into this question as they go through life trying to do right by the Black community on a daily basis. When you love someone, you want to do right by them even when it's hard to do right. The first theme that was evident from the responses of the YSBs was the need to uplift.

Ultimately, the best way to be responsibly Black is to do as Da Mayor said, *"Always do the right thing."* The doing the right thing includes understanding that actions and results mean much more than appearances and alibis. The doing the right things are doing those things that uplift the Black community.

Some of our YSBs suggest the best way to uplift is to do so directly, working in businesses or for causes explicitly designed to benefit the Black community. Other YSBs suggest that the best way to uplift the Black community is to provide it with an example of a life honorably lived.

This much is true. Our YSBs hold themselves accountable for the results of their lives and spend no time looking for scapegoats to blame for what they have not yet accomplished. They love their greatness more than they fear its price. However, as they decide how best to pursue greatness, they keep the best interests of the Black community in mind.

"Focus effort to help the Black community"

Many of our YSBs suggested the behavior that is responsible to the Black community means actually working within the Black community. This means creating businesses that serve the Black community directly, volunteering in some capacity within the Black community, or seeking to use one's position in another company to further the advancement of African Americans whenever possible. Even when the Black community does not fully embrace the help, our YSBs still felt strongly that they must continue to give it. According to these YSBs, there is not necessarily a right way to serve, but it is right to serve.

Forrest, 45, Director of Business Development

I indeed give to my community. I volunteer diligently in my neighborhood for the betterment of the Black community. Personally, I don't beat around the bush when I speak to my white counterparts regarding the Black functions I attend and the diversity within my own family, etc. On one occasion, I have "looked out" for my Brotha until I realized that he was not following through with me or his superiors. I was not about to be burned because of his lack of ability. I make sure I mentor other African-Americans in the corporate environment and align myself with the superiors (both Black and white) whom I admire and strive to be.

John, 38, Asst. Professor – Major, U.S. Army

I tried to go out of my way to attend Black movies, Black plays, spend time with Black youth, and mentor some Black college students. It is difficult to give help to people that don't want it. It is also difficult to explain to people that are not used to seeing a Black man help that I want to help them achieve their dreams. I have done some motivational speaking and joined some boards as well. I go out of my way (to reach out to the Black community) a lot because many young white men, young white women, and even foreign national or international students will seek out help from me on many things. Where are my young Black brothers and sisters? So I have to go out of my way to find them to tell them about my experiences, my offering of mentoring, scholarships, etc.

Janel, President, Financial Services Company

My mission for my company is to educate Black females on finances. Why? We are the foundation for our family and the future. If we don't understand our finances or how to make money grow, then we are going to fail our children, and financial ignorance will pass from generation to generation. Understanding our finances will break so many negative stereotypes and make our families and communities stronger as a whole.

"Serve the Black community by being a good example"

Within the Christian faith, many people are what steady churchgoers refer to as "Christmas-Easter Christians." These are people who show up at church on Christmas and Easter and are nowhere to be found the rest of the year. Some faithful Christians also deride those who appear holier than thou on Sunday but are raising hell Monday through Saturday. These "once-a-week Christians" are not walking the talk. They are hearing the sermon, but not living the sermon.

Many of our YSBs were careful to stress the importance of "living the sermon" with regard to the Black community. They place far more importance on being a person the Black community can be proud to emulate every day rather than one who simply seeks to look the part. One's "Blackness" or value to the Black community is not determined by the clothes one wears or even by where a person chooses to volunteer. The people who truly advance the cause of the Black community are the ones "living the sermon," living as an example of Black excellence for all to see every single day. These are the people who help soften hard hearts, change minds, break down doors, and inspire the next generation to do the same.

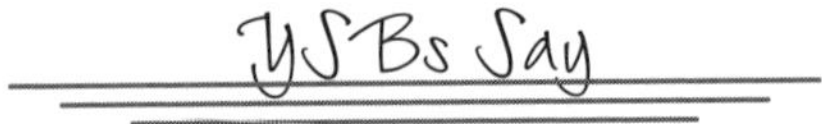

Gina, 28, Multimedia Specialist, Federal Government

I make sure that I try my best to live my life as a Christian first and I feel the rest will follow. People will respect me for my Christian behavior and there will be not much need to tailor my behavior. With that said, I do believe that I have a civic duty to vote and to participate in the political process. I do believe that my professionalism at work is being "documented" so my actions should speak much louder than anyone's perceived stereotypes of my community.

Monica, 38, Owner, Public Relations Firm

I continue to be who I am, an African-American woman who was raised, nurtured, and educated by a strong family who through their personal journeys have instilled in me a strong pride in my Black heritage. Now I do personally feel a sense of responsibility to showcase to the world the fact that African-Americans can do, can change, and can advance in this world. That, again, is the responsibility I have personally placed on myself because of who I am and how I was raised. Bottom line, what you see is truly what you get.

Shani, 35, Public Relations Consultant

Each situation calls for a different approach. As an African-American woman, I believe it is my responsibility to my community to represent myself to the highest level possible whether I am talking to a room full of white male oncologists or to room full of Southern-bred Baptists.

Bernadette, 29, Product Development, Fortune 100 Automotive Company

I tailor my behavior by being very proactive because I like to diffuse the stereotype that Blacks are lazy or always late. I participate in events that are not normal to me (deer hunting, skiing, euchre) to show that people in the Black community will try new things. Also, I speak proper English rather than using slang in the workplace and watch what I wear to outside events for the company. For example, I won't wear my Apple Bottom jeans or Baby Phat to a corporate picnic.

Krystal, 26, Registered Nurse / Travel Professional

I do find myself changing "coats." However, I feel there is a time and a place for everything. This includes loud voices, dancing, blunt sharing of opinions, etc. Professionalism is a major issue for me and though I represent the African-American community, my appearance would be clean and polished regardless of my race. However, I believe I must be an outstanding performer in order to reverse certain stereotypes associated with African-Americans.

Marvin, 38, President, Consumer Goods Company

I know I am Black and I am very proud of my heritage. I appreciate and realize the numerous struggles that we face as a race. I have faced many of those very struggles in my thirty-eight years of life. My outlook on life and the paths that I choose are based on what works for me and my family. I don't characterize my behavior(s) or opinions (personally, politically, or professionally) as simply "Black." My skin color or the race that I was born into does not define me. I am more than just a Black man that is a member of the Black community. I have more depth than that limited description. My mind does not accept such a closed view of the world in which I live.

Marc, 40, IT Implementation Manager

I try my best to be a role model to the younger generation (family, friends) as well as my colleagues at work. The younger set needs to see Black faces in important roles who can "hang" with the Black folks, yet also handle their business in the boardroom. They need to see someone who can be a standard-bearer within the company (on time or early, never outworked, respected by the other executives), yet still be "one of the people."

Kathy, 41, Business and Non-Profit Management Professional

I tailor my behavior as actor Laurence Fishburne depicted in the movie Deep Cover. When Fishburne, who portrayed a cop, was asked in an interview by a white law enforcement officer how he would react to being called the "N-word," his response was one that showed a sense of responsibility to the larger Black community. The interviewer indeed deserved to be slapped for the condescension, but his tactic had a purpose and motive. Laurence let him know that a true "N-word" would have jumped across the desk and whipped him down, yet he did not. He got the assignment because of his ability to rule his tongue and his temper.

I am smart enough, wise enough, and polished enough to know when to be "real Black" and when I must conduct myself in a matter that is beneficial to the (Black community) and not just myself. I also like to disappoint or shock people who expect all of "us" to act a certain way.

"Serve the Black community by being true to oneself"

With all the discussion about what is "real," the only real "real," according to many of our YSBs, is being true to oneself. The Black community is not served by people who support us out of obligation. Black people should be true to themselves and follow their hearts. They should serve the community only if their hearts compel them to do so. However, these YSBs stress that we must not harshly judge Blacks who do not hear this call. To thy heart, be true.

Joyce, 39, High School Principal

In general I don't tailor my behavior out of a sense of responsibility to the larger Black community because I feel that the best way to contribute to my race and the world is through being myself. However, I do make it a point to try to mentor and assist those of my same race in any way I can. For instance, in the work place, if there is a person of my race (and gender and similar upbringing) who's trying to get ahead and may need encouragement or opportunity, I will provide it if I can.

This does not mean that I neglect helping those of another race. It simply means that I acknowledge that as a person of color in this country, institutional racism and the status quo are such that racial minorities don't have equal access to opportunity. Minorities may not have had equity in education, social exposure, or exposure to cultural experiences, networking, or knowledge about the inner workings of a particular system. Thus, it is incumbent upon those successful persons or those who have an inroad of any sort to share the access and information they have with others. I see nothing wrong with this practice of mine at all. In fact, I see people of other races and genders doing it all the time.

Patrice, 22, Founder, New Media Company

I hold myself at a high standard educationally, professionally, socially, etc. I'd like to imagine that I can serve as a role model to young girls who are searching for pieces of themselves. I want to ensure that along the way they develop self-worth, pride, esteem, and vigor for life. I don't feel the need to have different versions of myself to suit certain situations because I feel that I live in a decent manner. I don't curse a lot when hanging out in the city, nor do I put on a phony French accent when I sometimes answer the phone at work. I am well-rounded and personable and don't have to change myself for situational purposes.

Now, of course, I act appropriately for each situation. I am not as loud as I may be with friends while at work, and not as talkative or silly in a meeting as I may be at other times. However, those adjustments are common sense adjustments due to me being aware of my surroundings and do not require any adaptation of the actual person that I am.

Natascha, 29, Career Coach

I don't tailor my behavior at all. I am who I am in my house, at work, speaking at an event, at a barbeque, or eating sushi at a five-star restaurant. If you behave differently in your "different worlds" eventually those "worlds" will collide at an unwanted time, so why act any differently? I choose to be polished 24/7. One of my mentors said to me, "Natascha, you are always on." At the time I was finishing my reign as Miss Black Rhode Island and I kept saying I am not "on" any longer—it's over. (The response I received to this comment was) "Natascha, you will always be that to us." Adults and children alike are always watching you. You've made a name for yourself, so remember "you are always 'on.'"

Tammy, 27, Business Owner, Fashion

I have a sense of responsibility to myself and my family. I think as Black people we tend to try and put on a show for each other and forget the person we are trying to impress may not even know who we are or even care.

Celebrity has taken over the minds of America and if you are not on TV or in a video you don't exist. I try to go out and work with kids with dreams and expose them to people such as myself. We are the mathematicians, scientists, teachers, etc. I can't change the mind of an old fool but I can make a hell of an impression on our youth. I think if you feel you have to tailor yourself for anyone's liking you don't know yourself and are wasting your time. Professionalism comes with the job and people are going to think of you any way they choose. My mom use to say, "They talked about Jesus Christ, so who the heck are you?"

CHAPTER TEN
WHO TO BE

If we, the Black community, are to be a more successful people, we need to build a more robust pipeline of successful individuals. A successful Black individual is someone who is guided by love. Show me a successful Black person and I will show you someone who loves himself or herself enough to pursue positive change rather than self-sabotaging by wallowing in negativity. This person will find a way to make something work even when faced with dozens of reasons why it will not. This person does not believe in "The Man" any more than he or she believes in the Tooth Fairy. This person uses hardships as lessons upon which to build success, not as proof that failure is inevitable. This person understands that greatness, and mediocrity, is a choice and, therefore, chooses wisely. This person loves himself or herself too much to accept mediocrity when we all deserve so much more.

Show me a successful Black person and I will show you someone who loves the Black community enough, loves you and me enough, to encourage our success. This successful Black person understands that he or she does not know everything there is to know about success or "Blackness," and therefore chooses not to pass judgment on either. This person has no time to hate because he or she is too busy spreading love. This person knows that our connection is deeper than skin tone, mate choice, or sartorial style.

Successful Black people know that anything that grows need to be fed well to stay strong, so they feed the Black community regularly. They understand that they are made stronger when you and I are strong. If it does not serve the Black community, a successful Black person is not saying it or doing it, no matter the "it." The stakes are simply too high.

The successful Black person knows one more prerequisite of our success as a Black community of which we must become aware. We must not only love ourselves enough to allow ourselves to be great and love each other enough to encourage our collective greatness. We must love our future generations enough to share our success lessons. Other groups known for their culture of success earn this success through a culture of knowledge sharing. These groups have found that by sharing their knowledge, the result is not simply additive, but multiplicative. By teaching one person the "tricks of the trade," you do not simply impact him but potentially his entire extended family or social circle. One young man or woman who, as a result of your counsel, goes to college rather than prison can change the outcomes of hundreds of lives. The young man or woman will have opportunity to be successful and then model that successful behavior for all with whom he or she comes in contact. The imperative to share your knowledge becomes all the more pressing when you remember that you are only where you are today, with your ability, your drive, and your wherewithal, because someone came into your life and helped you simply out of kindness. The imperative to share your love, to "pay it forward," is a moral imperative.

There is a practical reason to share your love as well. Show me anyone who we consider great and I will show you someone who puts others first. The greatest people among us, Black or otherwise, are the ones who have done the most for the most. Most often, we define greatness not by individual prowess, but by the depth and breadth of one's impact. An athlete's greatness is ultimately determined by championships won, not statistics tallied. A championship is a demonstration of collective success, of a great athlete's ability to make others better. A business person's greatness is determined by his or her impact on the bottom line, not personal salary dollars earned. The greatest business people are measured by the impact they had on the marketplace, the extent to which customers valued their products, and shareholders profited from their sale. A great business person brings the most value to the greatest number of people. A leader's greatness is determined by his or her ability to positively impact lives. The leaders we choose to follow and grow to love are the ones who changed the most lives for the better. The rewards for being great are many: money, power, fame, adulation, pride, satisfaction, and sometimes happiness. The rewards are many, but the price is simple. One must do for others to earn the spoils of greatness.

Who To Be

Spread love and you shall be rewarded. This is a lesson successful people know well. Therefore, it should come as no surprise that the YSBs surveyed for *Love Letter* were very willing to share their knowledge about being successful and Black. Sharing knowledge will only make us all stronger. In fact, this is the final lesson from our YSBs. Be generous with everything you know. The impact of your knowledge will not just add but multiply. Our YSBs had much advice regarding how to be successful and Black. I was enlightened and inspired both by what they said and what they didn't say. There was almost no mention of how to beat "The Man." Perhaps this was because "The Man" does not exist to successful Black people. YSBs do not believe they can be stopped, only contained for short periods of time.

What advice would you give to the aspiring "YSBs"?
What should they start or continue doing?
What should they stop doing?

Our YSBs gave us all much to ponder regarding being successful and Black when asked the "success question" above. Much of their advice centered upon "who to be." Success is a demonstration of character before it is a set of actions. Our YSBs argue that if you think successfully, your thoughts will become actions and your actions will become successful results. Who should you be? Our YSBs say we should all aspire to be someone who takes responsibility, demands excellence, learns from adversity, and consistently demonstrates a high moral character.

"Take responsibility"

No matter the area of discipline, the people we admire most take responsibility in all aspects of their lives. We admire the person who "steps up" to take blame more quickly than he or she seeks the credit. We admire someone who, in defeat, does not diminish the achievements of the victor by insisting the victory was somehow tainted or ill-gotten. We admire the person who can admit mistakes without qualification or equivocation. *"I'm sorry, but..."* is a non-apology that admirable people know better than to offer. Either you are sorry or you are not sorry. There is no in-between.

The ability to take responsibility even when one has a "good excuse," especially when one has a "good excuse," is not only admirable but empowering. We can step into our power to influence and control outcomes of our lives only when we become willing to own those outcomes. YSBs say that taking responsibility is the first thing the Black community must do.

Tammy, 27, Business Owner, Fashion Industry

I think as Black people we need to look beyond our government and look within ourselves. We have options. There's not going to be a miracle program that heals our minds and souls from slavery or society. We are the only solution. The healing comes from within, self-sufficiency. We need to start believing in ourselves more and stop being so negative. America doesn't need to know about all our internal cultural laundry. Some things are better left unsaid. Start your own businesses. Research and attend seminars. Support Black-owned businesses. Be professional. Manage your time well. Save and invest your career and community. Network and get an education (formally and informally). Learn to step outside the box. Don't run with the pack. Learn the industry you want to enter. Learn what your degree can do for you. Intern or volunteer while you are in high school. Don't let society label you or your thoughts. All Black people are not the same. Remember, America is not the only country doing business. Think globally and act locally. Invest money into politics (we need to put our money where our mouth is).

Bernadette, 29, Product Development, Fortune 100 company

Start taking advantage of every opportunity available to you because you never know to what it will lead. Continue to learn and educate yourself, be it formally or informally. Stop blaming others for your lack of success. You are in control of your own fate. Stop making it a Black and white thing. Most of the time, it's a people thing.

Nasiba, 32, Manager, Pharmaceutical Company

Continue to pursue your education and work as hard as you can to achieve your goals. Nothing worth keeping in life comes easy. Don't believe in rhetoric like "'The Man' keeps us down." Instead, do what is needed to become successful. Go into any job situation believing that you are the best person for the job. Racism exists everywhere, but does not exist in everyone. Stay true to who you are and always give back to the community from where you came. Inspire the life of a youngster by setting a good example with your success, and instill in them the proper steps to ensure their success.

Therone, 36, President, Publishing Company

I would definitely say study your history because if you don't know who you are then you do not know where you're going. Too many young Black people find themselves career-wise in that place where there might not be too many other Blacks. If you're not comfortable and sure in your own skin by yourself, how are you going to be amongst others? I would also say "grow up." When you get on that path to becoming successful, start playing the part beforehand. Leave the streets, the hood, and that whole attitude back there. You don't have to be a house Negro. But you do have to wise up about how to think and act because actions dictate the lives we live. Don't be that young cat that signed that million-dollar contract but got caught with a nine-millimeter and a bulletproof vest. Get around people that are either where you want to be or are on the same path as you. Get rid of friends, associates, and whoever else does not want you to be successful. You don't need anyone bringing you down because life is challenging enough. Take notes, make goals, have the end in mind. Once you complete a goal, move on to the next one. Challenge yourself to keep moving forward. Believe in God and believe in yourself.

Theresa, 44, Owner, Plumbing Company

First and foremost, get an education because it is the foundation to life. Without education, you will have struggles and difficulties and with it you have the stability of the Rock of Gibraltar. (Education will be a foundation that) can and will support anything you put on it. If you start something, complete the mission. Don't let anyone tell you what you cannot do because you are capable of doing whatever you want. You will only be as successful as you want to be. It is in your hands.

To my young Black sisters, stop with the multi-color hair weaves, as job opportunities will only pass you by. Let's dress a little more appropriately leaving something to the imagination. Most importantly, learn to respect yourself. To my young Black brothers, by all means, please pull up the pants and quit showing the butt. Any time you dress like this, remember it could be your mother or grandmother you're disrespecting.

Please realize at some point in time everyone will have a story to tell about their lives. Why not make yours an exciting one?

Tangela, 27, Community Legal Advocate

Be who you are, don't let anyone tell you that, in order to succeed, you have to look or act a certain way. Be proud to speak correctly and dress everyday like a professional. I live by the Marianne Williamson quote, "Your playing small doesn't serve the world. There's nothing enlightened about shrinking so that other people won't feel insecure around you…And as we let our light shine, we unconsciously give other people permission to do the same."

Shalom, 36, Author

To my young, successful brothers and sisters who are up and coming: Set some goals for yourself. Focus on your passion, study it, perfect your skills in it, network with others who are already successful in it (not necessarily all, but especially Blacks), and put your plans into action. Stop making excuses, PLEASE. Nobody's seriously stopping you but YOU.

Tracey, 38, Public School Teacher

Don't try to be something that you're not. Learn to listen to yourself intuitively, gain spiritual grounding—pray, chant, meditate—and do something good that will propel you into good. Aim to not repeat generational setbacks (abuse, despair, poverty, negative behavior/thoughts). Appreciate your shortcomings and aspire to be a person you would like to know and have in your life. Goodness is possible. Understand your purpose and unique calling in life by allowing yourself to travel in different circles of people and getting to know other cultures, religions, neighborhoods, cities, states, countries. Don't grow yourself in a box of what you already know—GROW! Know that to whom much is given, much is expected!

Rod, 42, College Instructor

Understand the path you are traveling. The path was traveled before you by ordinary people who accomplished extraordinary things. Young people must continue laying the foundations for the generations that will follow them. Also, you must share the three T's: Talent, Time, and Treasure.

Lee, 48, Founder, Apparel Company

We are all purpose providers. The urgency to revive the power of our people in unity to achieve higher levels of academic and professional successes for our youth is obvious. Spread the colors. Share the message. And encourage any and everyone to do their part.

Lucretia, 31, Community Activist

My advice is that life is what you make it—so you have to make life worth living. Live your dream and follow your heart. Set the standards for yourself. Don't give up no matter what comes your way. My favorite scripture, Jeremiah 29:11, reads; "for I know the plans I have for you, plans to prosper you and not to harm you, plans to give you hope and a future."

Oscar, 37, Entertainment Industry Consultant

A wise friend told me what I would tell aspiring YSBs. "You can make moves or excuses, but not both." Stop waiting for your shot. Take it. Then watch where it lands, pick it up, reload, aim, and take a better shot. Here is the "new" mantra for YSBs. It's not "ready, aim, fire," but "ready, fire, aim." Now spend every waking moment getting and staying "ready" for success. I wish you fortune (not "luck," because I have faith)!

Kendall, 30s, Writer / Founder, Production Company

I don't like to advise a group of people on "should" or "should not" for individual lives. I don't prescribe to group mentalities or group identities because it strips people of their individuality. The same holds true in our writing workshops when someone offers, "You should get rid of this or that character," or "You shouldn't write this story using third person limited POV." Creativity is a unique fingerprint, just as a personality, temperament, or being left or right-handed.

I believe that some African Americans suffer from a "crabs in the barrel" mentality. We are a multi-faceted, hued, and talented people. One size doesn't fit all, and the sooner we accept this fact, the better off we will be.

"Demand excellence of yourself"

So often we become who we expect to be. If this is true, why not expect greatness? We can no longer afford to excuse poor behavior or performance with the phrase, "You know how Black folks are." We can no longer assume that mediocrity is our goal and any higher achievement is gravy. We cannot continue to grade ourselves on a discounted scale of excellence. True excellence is only excellence acceptable. We must begin to expect this of ourselves, starting with the "man in the mirror."

Crystal, 45, Manager, Fortune 100 Consumer Products Company
First and foremost, get an education, keep your minds strong (staying away from drugs), and learn how to stay financially strong. Don't attempt to "get it all at once" and reach for fame and glory without putting in some dues or even hard work. Nothing comes without an investment. Go after your passion. Plan how this passion can make you successful. Read often and read at all levels (newspapers, novels, and industry news). Do what you do well and, finally, incorporate into your plan how you can give back or give to others.

Eddie, 49, Business Owner, Consulting

First and foremost, get knowledge! Your first order of business is to be able to provide for yourself and family. Next, follow your passion no matter what the naysayers have to say. Embrace failure, learn from it, and use it as a platform upon which you may build toward your ultimate success.

John, 43, Managing Partner, Consulting

I would encourage aspiring YSBs to gain a thorough understanding of the objectives of the organization/group/division/team. I would then encourage them to keep that in mind and how to help the company achieve it. I would encourage thought leadership. He/she should understand "where the rubber meets the road," or, better yet, how the company makes money. With that understanding, proceed to drive those results. Additionally, be slow to reveal your entire self. You can always roll out additional information about yourself. However, you can never have a recall once it is out. You get to create your own image based on what you give them to ponder.

Tracy, 49, Sr. Sales Manager, Fortune 100 Consumer Products Company

There is a time for being yourself and a time for acting in a professional, responsible manner. Upon joining an organization, get on the schedule of the key individuals in the organization to both gain knowledge about the company and position and to build a personal and professional relationship. I am convinced that people get ahead by having a mentor and/or sponsor to support and help advise them on their careers. When in a business setting, talk business and show others you know about and want to learn more about the company and your position. Many people think we only know about "sports," for example, and will pigeon-hole us into that mindset. Show them you know and care about a broad array of business topics.

Earsell, 44, Sales Manager, Fortune 100 Consumer Products Company

Start doing: Prepare for war in time of peace. Make sure you have options. Always remember that the same rules do not apply to you, no matter how successful you are within any organization. Choose you battles and understand not every situation is worth fighting for.

Continue doing: Support your community and family. Always reach back and help someone. Be a mentor. Continue to stay strong, and never let them see you sweat. Keep cool. Keep your business as your business.

Stop doing: Blaming things on "The Man." If he tries to stop you, go around him, but do it in a respectful way that is professional.

James, 37, VP, Financial Services Company

Build a technical skill that matters. Stay away from being a generalist. It may take time to identify and hone this skill, but be mindful that over time it helps to have expertise in something. Think like an owner versus a consumer. Save, Save, Save! Pick up credentials early (MBA, CFA, Master's, etc.). Travel the world when possible. Have strong non-minority mentors as well.

Marc, 40, IT Implementation Manager

I would tell them to develop friends/colleagues outside of their normal circles as early in life as possible. While they may join a Black fraternity/sorority in college, they can also join a business fraternity. Foster these friendships as they can be great bridges to a successful career. They also need to find mentors in the corporate world who can help them traverse the often rocky landscape. The corporate world is rarely straightforward and if you don't understand the ins and outs, you can be swept aside very quickly. Learning about things such as aligning yourself with the right individuals, networking within the proper groups, building your network base outside of work, even which after-work functions are not really "voluntary," can go a long way helping you get to the next level.

I also implore people when they get into an organization to study the environment and then act accordingly. You should know fairly quickly what it will take to have success in that organization if you follow their blueprint. Don't think that you can "do it your way" and still achieve the same things. Once you know the corporate culture, accept it. Understand that if you don't live within that culture that certain things just will not happen for you there. That may not be a bad thing because you may not be looking to ascend the corporate ladder, but know this going in so that you don't end up bitter down the road.

Monique, 40, Manager

Education and knowledge is power. When you have that, you can do and be whatever and whoever you want to be. You are no longer a color. You are a smart and educated person. Access is success.

Torin, 39, Business Owner, Executive Search

Do this: Portray yourself as an exceptionally smart tactician. People are drawn to those who execute delivery in a natural, effortless way.

Continue this: 1) reading a range of topics/writers, 2) networking with passion, and 3) thinking as an entrepreneur. Bringing bandwidth and high-speed access will set you atop. Being available and able to generate cross-directional attention drives others to create feelings about you that develop over time. Time builds trust. Trust increases your buzz. Learn to speak with others about a compelling future that overshadows their past.

Easy to do: 1) ask a question, 2) listen, and 3) ask another question. Repeat over and over again. This brings breakthroughs for you and those you encounter! The second response: Stop making excuses!

Carmen, 27, Publicist

Aspiring YSBs should stop being afraid to take a risk. They should reach out to mentors, not only mentors who look like them but mentors who are where they want to be in life. YSBs should support each other and only speak and behave positively when interacting and doing business with one another. Aspiring YSBs should hit the ground running in unconventional ways when job searching. They should set up informational interviews, lunch dates, meetings, etc. with those they might want to work alongside one day. They should keep the faith, declare, confess, and claim their success. They should surround themselves with people who enrich and enlighten their lives. They should do what they say they are going to do and follow through with flying colors. They should continue to work twice as hard for a blessing rewarded two-fold.

Aspiring YSBs should take the initiative and pursue professional development. They should expand their social circles to those who don't look like them to learn and grow. This will make them even more appealing and educated in a global economy. YSBs should travel, study, and work abroad. They should learn foreign languages and embrace other cultures. The more unique we are, the more we move forward and stand out. Most importantly,

YSBs need to remember the other African Americans who helped them achieve their success. They should NEVER hesitate to assist young people in need of motivation.

Brian McClellan

"Learn from adversity"

Successful people make a lot of mistakes. However, they rarely repeat their mistakes. Part of the "genius" of successful people is the courage to replay negative outcomes in their minds with the purpose of getting better. I place the word "genius" in quotes because one does not have to be smart to learn from experience, only diligent. Life is a tremendous teacher. The most successful people among us live life as if school is always in session.

Our YSBs spoke often about having the courage to learn from adversity. Often, we can be successful but have no idea why what we are doing is working. Sometimes we need to fail to understand what actions are necessary for success. In fact, the most successful people among us will often intentionally place themselves in difficult situations to hasten the learning process. If you want to have more success, they argue, make more mistakes. Remember, school is always in session. Don't miss a single class.

YSBs Say

Dwight, 28, Business Owner, Financial Services

My suggestion to YSBs would be, "never give up on your dreams." If you don't believe in yourself no one else will either. And most importantly, always try to turn a negative situation into a positive one. Bad or good, make it a learning experience. For instance, my nephew was killed at seventeen years of age due to senseless violence. As much as it hurt to bury a nephew I watched grow from a baby to a young man, the positive in that situation was that it opened my eyes and helped me get my act together so I could prevail. We watch murder victims' families on the news every day, but as humans we tend to believe at times it can't happen to us until it hits home. I say all this to say that in every bad thing that happens to us there is a good somewhere in between.

Also, surround yourself with those that have the same goals as you and can enhance your growth. Take the three people who are around you the most and average their incomes. That will become your (income).

Janel, President, Financial Services Company

I will tell every YSB to gain as much knowledge as possible about their finances. If it's success you desire, failure is unavoidable. But understand that they must find the silver lining in every mistake and take it as a learning opportunity. Setbacks and failure must NEVER discourage you. Take the time to learn how to build your business credit. Proper preparation prevents poor performance—you might only have one opportunity. Stop listening to people who are not where you want to be. Find a mentor in your industry and network, network, network. Once you have made it, ALWAYS reach back and help the next YSB.

"Adopt a strong personal character"

YSBs believe that good things happen to and for good people. The people who give of their time and talents generously to others receive the benefits ten-fold. They attract the people, resources, and support they need to be successful. People want to help people who are willing to help others. Success finds people who work hard, work long, and work honestly. Our YSBs believe those who work to be people worthy of emulation will have success worthy of admiration.

Our YSBs in their responses understand that success begins in the mind. Therefore, much of their advice describes the person we should aspire to be. By working everyday to be this person, we will put ourselves in a position to be successful. By becoming who we should be, we can begin to have what we should have.

Fred, 45, Pastor

Aspiring YSBs should:

1. Build a relationship with God, the strongest foundation that one can have, and then build genuine relationships with others upon that solid foundation. Be willing to support, encourage, and hold one another accountable to be the very best.

2. Maintain integrity in all endeavors and remain objective and willing to learn from anyone who has something of value to teach.

3. Invest in others. Always remember that nothing we possess ever reaches its fullest potential (skill, money, knowledge, love, etc.) until it's shared or given away.

4. Commit to achieving excellence and strive to make a significant contribution for all humanity.

5. Collaborate as well as compete. Do not allow your passion to succeed overshadow your compassion for others.

6. Be willing to "grow through" whatever challenges you have to "go through."

7. Be intentional about enjoying the journey!

Kevin, 33, VP, Banking Company

The first thing YSBs should start doing is to believe in themselves. Throughout life, a person may have several opportunities to fail or succeed, but the key to long-lasting success is to maintain self-confidence and to stay focused. I also believe that there is nothing wrong with secondhand experience. If a YSB can find a mentor that they consider successful and can learn from this mentor's mistakes and successes, then this could shorten the time it takes for them to reach their success goals. Finally, my advice to YSBs is to stop making decisions based solely on what are the most popular choices at the current time. Make well thought out decisions based on facts, circumstances, and how those choices can fit into their overall plan for success.

Shonika, 35, Pioneer of Youth & Teen Entrepreneur Coaching

Aspiring YSBs should start breaking their self-defeating cycle by reading and by truly seeing to helping people, including themselves. When I say truly helping people, I mean generously giving your peers valuable and useful information without asking or implying that you want anything in return. I mean openly sharing resources and connecting the people in your network. Nobody is going to try to cheat you unless, in the back of your mind, you are countering how you will beat them to the punch. When you focus that negative energy on what others are trying to do to get over on you, then you act out of this negativity, thus making the other person suspicious of you. Then you both fight for assets (what little there probably are) and ultimately cheat each other. You enter the next opportunity with the same mindset about other people and you continue to repeat the cycle. You should be so confident and open in giving information and resources that you could share those things with "your competitors."

Read the great sales and marketing books dating back to the early twentieth century from the likes of Napoleon Hill and the Carnegies of the world. They did not see themselves as having competitors. They saw themselves as the best darn person at whatever they did and essentially their competitors saw them as a resource. They seek to learn from others rather than duplicate their efforts. This is essentially how franchises are successful in the offline world and how information marketers are successful in the online world. Someone came up with the great idea and they say "I have already done the trial and error, so you can save a lot of time and money by just doing what I did." (The franchise fee charged) is how much that time saved and intellectual property gained is worth.

Translate this to your personal life as well. You will be amazed by the return you will get on your investment when you learn to let go of your inhibitions and old school ideologies, have good follow through, and let the universe handle the rest.

Dwight, 46, Insurance Professional

The YSBs should continue to be leaders in the community. They should continue to step outside the box. They should continue to reach back and help those who are less fortunate without feeling obligated. It should come from the heart. They should pass on their talent to their children. In addition, we all should not always think about leaving money to our kids. Leaving a talent will carry them further than money. Let's talk to our kids about what they should do. Show them what they should do. We should be more visible in the schools (especially men). I used to run an after school program. The biggest problem I had was lack of parental participation in the schools. We were only going to the school when our child got in trouble or suspended.

YSBs, stay in your child's business. You are obligated to know what is going on in your child's life at all times. If you stay involved their lives, you can see trouble coming and stop it before it is too late. We are all obligated to make sure our children will be able to survive in the real world. This means we must teach them to respect people, follow rules, and take them to church. If they do not know how to follow rules and the consequences of breaking the rules as a child, the consequences of breaking the rules in the real world could have a lifetime effect. We should stop allowing our kids to do what they want. Act like a parent! This is our job! Our jobs as a parents starts on day one, not at age twelve.

We should stop criticizing each other. We should stop mistreating our women. We should stop calling Blacks "sellouts." I believe money only magnifies one's personality. If a person is stingy before he gets rich, he will be stingy after he gets rich. If a person has a giving heart before he gets rich, he will have a giving heart after he gets rich. We can be difference makers. Change will happen whether we want it to or not. Why not be responsible for the changes? Let's increase the network among Black people. It is time we started to trust each other. It is time we learned to coexist without envy. The future is now. I DO NOT KNOW WHAT TOMORROW HOLDS, BUT I DO KNOW WHO HOLDS TOMORROW.

Selvin, President, Diversity Consulting Firm

I would tell all young men and women to study their dreams, act on their visions, develop ideas, formulate plans, implement planned strategies, and always remain receptive to change. Develop your own mechanisms to drive internal motivation because it builds intestinal fortitude to brave life's many battles. Do not fixate on race or ethnicity, age, or any physically distinguishing characteristic. Focus on your own strengths.

Gina, 28, Multimedia Specialist, Federal Government

Start out being a good (person) first and the rest will follow. Have people respect you first and then they will have one more positive image of a YSB. My other piece of advice is to help each other out and don't "hate." We get ourselves nowhere by infighting, so we should do our best to work together. Definitely don't bring your emotional baggage into the workplace. Don't make people feel uncomfortable around you because they're afraid that you might blow up thinking that someone's being racist. If someone disrespects you, then find another way to let them know. Diversify. Diversify. Diversify.

That means your educational and international experience. Learn at least a basic level of some foreign language. These things can take you a LONG way in making yourself a well- rounded candidate for success!

Kathy, 41, Business and Non-Profit Management Professional

I advise all YSBs to use proper English, get the best education they can when afforded to them, and to network heavily with those who are doing better than they or doing what they wish to do. Additionally, getting a mentor is very helpful. They should stop feeling threatened by other YSBs who seem to be doing better or have more. Partner with them to learn how to achieve the same. Do not undermine "your people" or work against them to bring them down. We have enough opposition to do that for us already.

Lawrence, 29, Benefits Coordinator, Non-Profit Education Company

YSBs should always respect those who came before them. By doing this, there is a sense of responsibility to those who came before you or those who pushed you to where you are. This sense of responsibility is best played out by giving back and by bringing others along with you. If you're the only success in your family, it makes one question what you have given back to ensure that others are learning as well.

Many people get caught up in the "crabs in a barrel" syndrome. The moment they get close to getting out, someone pulls them down…and usually it isn't even physically. Once they allow themselves to fall victim to the words of others and see someone else's success, their own bitterness for falling victim earlier makes them a victimizer.

Don't allow the opinions of others prevent your success. You can't make everyone happy, but at least if you can make yourself happy you have won more than half the battle. Don't become embittered by your slower growth and someone's faster acceleration. You don't know what their sacrifices were and their step out might allow for your step up. Don't change your goal, even when the path to it may have to be adjusted. Flexibility in achieving your goal will help you achieve it.

Melvin, 38, President, Venture Capital Firm

Be true to yourself. Adapt to the dominant culture when necessary, but don't lose yourself. Look out for people who "look like you." Always do the best you can.

Candace, 39, Financial Consultant

1. Money isn't everything. Don't take a job just because of the income. Find a balance. Do what you love to do. There is nothing like Peace in the Valley.

2. Don't be a militant. It will hurt you in the long run.

3. Keep your personal business to yourself. Keep them guessing.

4. Decide what is most important in your life. Is it family first, or job first, or personal life first? (After you decide what is most important) concentrate on making it happen.

Forrest, 45, Director of Business Development

Our intelligence is not dictated by our voice pattern, dialect, or the schools we attended. Be strong in who you are as a person, as an African American, as a man, as a woman, and as an aspiring YSB. Earn respect, don't demand it. Choose your battles, but do not settle for ignorance.

CHAPTER ELEVEN
HOW TO BE

Our YSBs offered some excellent advice regarding "who to be." We have to take responsibility for our successes and our failures in life. We must focus much more on "doing right," that is, taking the right actions to be successful rather than "being right" about racism. We must learn from adversity. Successful people are greedy and then generous with life's lessons. They are greedy for knowledge, always insisting that every life experience makes them better in some way. Then they are generous in that they share this knowledge with anyone and everyone. We must demand excellence of ourselves. Those who expect to win and prepare to win generally win. Winning is habit-forming and successful people simply can't kick the habit. Finally, we must conduct ourselves with the highest of moral character. This is strong advice, but how should we apply this knowledge? Now that we know "who to be" as Black individuals, we must answer the next question of "how to be." How do we best serve the Black community? What should be our guiding principle? Do you have to ask?

Love is the answer. Love is the mindset we must adopt. Love is our salvation as a Black community. It is love that will cause us to love ourselves as individuals enough to allow our greatness. Our greatness has been buried under challenges we were unsure we could meet and fears of what "they" would and would not allow. We know better now than to place fear above love. We know that love is stronger than fear, stronger than hate.

It is love that will cause us to love each other enough to uplift each other, to be the answer for each other rather than another question. We have been lost in the wilderness of intramural competition, distracted by squabbles over petty differences. Love will show us that that which unites us is far stronger than that which divides us. Love will show us that are interests are aligned, our destinies linked, and we are far greater together than we could ever be alone.

It is also love that will cause us to change the world in which our children and their children will live. We will be the generation to end slavery for the final time, the slavery of the mind. Love will ensure that our children will live free. Love will show us the way.

We know that love is the answer, but what should we do next? How will we translate the thoughts of love to the actions of love? How will we love our way to greatness as Black individuals and as a Black community?

Do What You Love – Select a Mission

A great people are comprised of many great individuals. The Black community needs more great individuals. Great individuals do what they love to do. They go through life "on a mission." Therefore, the Black community needs you to become a "missionary." Enduring greatness is not found in people who labor without love regardless of the size of their talent. Talents requires love to shape it. One needs to know in which direction to point his or her talent in order to be great. Ask yourself, "What is that thing for which I will pay the price of greatness?" What is that thing for which you will become single-minded, willing to do more, learn more, be more than the competition? Love holds the answer. Talent requires love to push it.

The difference between great and good, between good and mediocre, is more often "will" than "skill." One's will rather than one's skill is often the difference between winning and losing, success and failure. Your will causes you to consider all the angles prior to the big event. Your will causes you to anticipate trouble so well that when someone tries to throw a monkey wrench in your program, you have the answer, two answers, three answers, more answers than they have monkey wrenches. This type of will is love-driven. Love will give you the strength to press on when others would quit. Talent requires love to find a way around obstacles for which talent alone is no answer. Greatness is not easy. Greatness is tough to achieve, but love will make you tougher. Love will make you willing to fail one hundred times in order to taste sweet success on your one hundred and first try. Want greatness? Get love.

Need an example? See MJ. Michael Jordan was "Michael Jordan" because of love. There were basketball players who were more talented physically than Michael Jordan. Other players came and went during Air Jordan's reign who were faster runners or higher jumpers or more accurate shooters, but no one loved basketball, correction—winning basketball games, more than Michael Jordan. He loved winning basketball games enough to do the work to transform himself from an average shooter to an excellent shooter. He loved winning basketball games enough to seek less individual success in order to enable the success of his teammates because he knew strong teammates make winning basketball teams. He loved winning games enough to do the thankless work of playing defense as fiercely as he did the glamorous work of scoring points. He loved winning enough to avoid all of the temptations readily available to star athletes that prevent winning. Jordan didn't settle for being "good" when he was just good. He wanted to be great. When he became great, he wanted to be immortal. When so many of his peers were busy smelling themselves and getting too high off the scent to focus upon self-improvement, Jordan did the work of greatness. His love was as great as his talent and as a result there was no one better…ever.

Your individual greatness will depend upon what you choose to do. Greatness equals the product of talent and love. You can't be great without talent or love. Anything times zero is zero. However, your love will amplify your talent. This is the greatness equation. Before we understand the "greatness equation," we are tempted to choose our vocation strictly on our most obvious talent. Good at math? Become an engineer or accountant. Good at science? Become a doctor. Before we understand the greatness equation, we are tempted to select our life's work based upon the job that pays the most at the moment. You may be tempted to choose a vocation rather than a mission, which is a big mistake. Eventually you will learn that a bad job is a bad job no matter how much it pays. You will still come to despise it. At this moment, you will understand the power of the equation.

If you find yourself in a bad job, please know that your mission and your greatness still await you. There is a mission out there for you that can wake you up in the morning fired up, work you all day long, and then send you to bed with a smile on your face. Please know that the only way to be wildly successful is to embark upon a mission for which you need no outside prompting. Please know that the only way to be great at something is to be doing something for which in your mind, as Shalamar sang, *"there ain't no maybes. It's for the lover in you, baby."* Your greatness will depend upon when, or whether, you choose love. If you didn't know, now you know.

Our greatness as a Black community will depend on two extremely important choices you will make. Choice No.1 – What will you choose to do? Will you point your talent in the right direction? Will you choose something at which you were talented enough to win and you love enough to win? Both are required. If you have not placed yourself at the intersection of your talent and your love, you will not enjoy enduring greatness. Choose wisely.

However, the success of the Black community hinges upon your second choice. Choice No. 2 – Will you choose something that serves the Black community? Your greatness serves the Black community if it creates opportunity for the Black community. You benefit all of us by working directly to solve an issue by which Blacks are plagued. You serve us all if your greatness affords you disposable income to invest in the Black community. You serve us all if your greatness allows you time to invest in the Black community, an investment of your hands, your mind, or your heart. You serve us all if your greatness allows the door of opportunity to open a crack or swing open widely for someone else in the Black community. You serve us all if your greatness allows you to be an inspiration to someone else, anyone else, in the Black community seeking their own greatness. You serve us all if your greatness adds rather than subtracts, creates value rather than destroying it, create resources rather than draining them. You serve us all if your greatness makes us better in some way, be it large or small. There are infinite ways to serve, but it is essential that you serve. It is essential we all serve.

Can you imagine how powerful the Black community would be if thousands, hundreds of thousands, or millions more of us were "on a mission?" Even one single person on a mission is a force with which to be reckoned. Black history has been shaped by the stories of the unstoppable power of single individuals on a mission. Is there anything we could not do if we had thousands or millions of missionaries? We could change the course of history again. We could achieve as much as our collective imaginations will allow. We could bring about a new world order. We could knock the Earth off of its orbit. The change we would produce is incalculable. The Black community needs missionaries. Will you accept the mission?

Show Your Love – Share Your Mission

How will you know if you are doing the right thing? How will you know if you are on the right mission and therefore on your way to greatness? You will know if you can't wait to share your good news, to tell everyone who will listen about your mission. If you are doing what you were born to do, you won't be able to help yourself. You will be evangelizing and proselytizing all over the place. You'll be like the newlyweds who are so in love that they make everyone around them sick by always talking about their love and showing their love. You will know you are in the right place when you fall in love with your mission, marry it, and want to have babies with it.

Three very important benefits occur when you begin to evangelize about your mission. The first is that you become accountable for achieving the mission. Too often we have dreams that we don't share with folks because we are afraid of what they will say about them. We fear our dreams are too fragile to be exposed to the harsh outside elements, thus we prefer to keep them in the safe, climate-controlled space between our ears. We want to harbor these dreams in secret and work on them in seclusion until we are sure they will come true. Then and only then will we spring them on the world. By hiding our dreams, however, we make them much less likely to come true. By talking about your dreams, you become accountable to the people you tell. The people you tell will ask you again and again about your grand plans and you will want to be able to give them good news. The desire to please will provide you with much needed motivation.

Secondly, when you begin to share your mission with people, even your naysayers will help you make it come true. Haters sometimes serve an important role in making dreams come true. Often they make you aware of holes in your plan that are not insurmountable but for which you had not accounted. The haters can actually help you tighten up your game if you can listen past the hate to hear the message. The haters can also provide much needed motivation if you use them correctly. There will be a time when your fire for your mission will start to wane. At this moment, the thought of a hater will stoke it again. You will not want to give that hater the satisfaction of being right, so you will press on.

Finally, evangelizing about your mission will also do something else positive toward making it come true. By sharing your love for your mission, you will start to attract the help you need to make it a reality. People are attracted to those who are passionate about their work or their cause. We just can't help it. If you are on the right mission, your love for that mission will be contagious. You will attract the people, the information, the resources, and the support you need to make it successful. If you let people know what you are doing and expose them to your passion, you will find people who want to be a part of your winning team.

The Black community has many built-in vehicles for sharing information. We gather like no other people in the world gather. We gather at churches, college homecomings, family reunions, fraternity and sorority events, and professional organization events. We have no problem getting a bunch of us together at one time. We have a tremendous network we could employ to educate each other, a network which too often is allowed to stay dormant. We have the equivalent of trillions of barrels of oil under our surface that we fail to pump. We could use our gatherings, our built-in networks, much more effectively to share our missions.

Why not use the family reunion, for example, as an opportunity to educate ourselves on the principles of success? Someone at that reunion knows the importance of building wealth, for example, and can teach the basics. Someone knows the Rule of 72, someone knows the difference between individual stocks and mutual funds, and someone knows something about health care insurance. And many of the people in attendance do not. Why not use this opportunity to pass knowledge from loved one to loved one?

This is how successful groups of people do "family business." They get strong and stay strong by making sure that every individual in the group has access to the knowledge of the entire group, not just their own. Why are we so dedicated to our silence on the very issues that will make us healthier, wealthier, and wiser? Why not dedicate an hour or two of a weekend-long event to make ourselves a stronger people? If we cannot demonstrate our love by sharing information with our immediate families, how can we hope to collaborate to the degree we must as a Black community to change our world?

Make Your Love Eternal – Monetize Your Mission

A grave disservice that we do to each other in the Black community, and in society as a whole, is to attach a negative connotation to building wealth. This is an odd phenomenon to see in a nation that is the world's leading proponent of capitalism. However, even as we all pursue our brass rings, there is a simultaneous undercurrent of negativity toward those who achieve monetary success. Many politicians have made successful careers for themselves by ginning up animosity between economic classes and exploiting the resultant divide for their own personal gain. As a result, many people from all ethnicities believe that those who are wealthy, by definition, have exploited or taken advantage of those who are not wealthy to earn that wealth. They become trapped in the Catch-22 of being simultaneously envious of those who achieve financial success but ambivalent toward bringing their own financial success to fruition.

This problematic attitude is compounded within the Black community in two dangerous ways. Many Blacks believe that monetary success, especially when achieved in a corporate environment, implies that the successful person has been treasonous to the Black community. Therefore, many Black who want to "stay Black" are forced to choose between love of success and love of community and often end up failing on both counts.

Secondly, Blacks are increasingly embracing the "mythology of blingology," a culture that values having money, or appearing to have money, rather than building wealth. Many of the images with which the Black community is bombarded are of athletes and entertainers flaunting money and spending it indiscriminately. Worse still, we create many of these images ourselves and star in the "ads" for them. We are the ones creating a persistent message that encourages us to squander our resources rather than investing them or, better still, reinvesting them into Black communities. We are so fixated on the visual impact of "making it rain" that we fail to understand the power of the transaction. We fail to realize that while the "rainmaker" throws his bills skyward, the person who paid the "rainmaker" has his money working overtime. There is a distinct difference between having money and being wealthy. We need to be about building wealth.

Rather than trivializing the power of money by believing its only purpose is to feed a hedonistic lifestyle, we must learn to harness its power for the greatest good. The best way to advance the missions we choose to adopt as a community is to "monetize" those missions. The call to "reinvest in the Black community" has been repeated so often it is now a cliché, an empty promise that seems to motivate little positive action. The truest form of reinvestment would be to "monetize our missions," the Black community supporting missions to which we have chosen to dedicate our lives. How? By designing economic transactions that have the threefold purpose of bringing value to the marketplace with the products sold or services provided, bringing profit to the business owner, and bringing benefit to the Black community at large. This is "monetizing the mission" defined.

Why is monetizing the mission so important? Monetizing the mission is the only sure way to make sure our most important missions live in perpetuity. Too often, we in the Black community find ourselves in a position in which we must rely on charity to solve a problem or sometimes even to meet a basic need of our community. This is a dangerous strategy as charity is finite because resources are finite. Money and time are not unlimited, so at some point the givers of money and time must stop giving, leaving those who rely on the gift in deep trouble. We see this situation play out, for example, with the food banks that serve inner cities all over the country. Many people, often Black people, come to rely upon food banks to stretch their incomes to make ends meet. The mission of the food bank, of course, is to feed as many hungry people as possible. However, in difficult economic times, the number of people who need the mission to succeed increases while the charitable support the mission receives decreases. Charity is good and noble and everyone should give when they can. Unfortunately, charity is never an enduring solution to any problem. As long as charities require finite resources to operate, charity, by definition, will always end at some point and the mission of the charity will end as well.

Now contrast the food bank situation with a case in which a mission is monetized by its ability to generate income internally. A perfect example of a self-supporting mission is a private university. Private universities, first and foremost, are businesses. They sell access to knowledge and credentialing that has real value in the marketplace. The credential maintains its value because it cannot be simply purchased but must be earned through hard work and high achievement. The graduates who are able to earn these credentials will graduate with skills that are valuable to their potential employers and business partners. This trade, dollars for skills, is the transaction that private universities try to make as profitable as possible.

However, the most successful private universities do not stop earning money after they have collected tuition payments and fees from their students. These private universities also have highly capable and extremely sophisticated fund-raising organizations that actively solicit charitable contributions. The mission embedded in the business of the private school is to ensure it can continue providing a high-quality education to students forever. To that end, the fund-raising arms of the most successful of these universities have created endowments valued in the tens of billions of dollars. These endowments are professionally managed and generate tremendous income in their own right, providing a bulletproof hedge against "hard times" the university may face. The entity makes money internally and therefore the mission can live forever. Any charity this entity receives is not its sole reason for being, but rather serves to make its mission more secure. With the tremendous amount of talent and buying power we have within our community, we certainly have the wherewithal to create "monetized missions" to benefit our community.

Would this work in the Black community? We are already doing it. One such "monetized mission" within the Black community is a business called Food From the Hood (FFTH). In 1992, students from Crenshaw High School in Los Angeles turned an abandoned lot behind a football field into a two-acre vegetable garden from which the FFTH business grew. Today, Food From the Hood has grown into a business that sells vegetables and bottled salad dressings to two thousand stores nationwide while still donating a quarter of the product of the garden to local citizens in need. Perhaps the best part of FFTH business is that it is managed locally by student managers who do so in return for scholarship dollars. To date, $250,000 in scholarship funds have been awarded to the student managers, funding the college education of seventy-seven students. Embedded in the business of selling salad dressings are the dual missions of feeding local families and funding the higher education of local students.

The students who work for Food From the Hood are getting an education much more valuable than the scholarship dollars they have earned. Even more importantly, the survival of the Food From the Hood enterprise is not predicated upon society's willingness to give charitably but instead on FFTH's ability to produce quality salad dressings that consumers value. As long as FFTH continues to run a profitable business that meets customer needs, students will continue to learn the value of hard work, gain entrepreneurial and leadership skills, and have funds available to further their educations while local families will be fed. In other words, the mission will live on. FFTH can live forever as a business entity and in spirit through the good works of its graduates.

Is there any reason there cannot be a Food From the Hood, or five or ten, in every major metropolitan area in the country? Of course, they would not all be selling vegetables and salad dressings, but every one of them could be creating valuable transactions that ultimately invest in our future. We are certainly capable enough to create hundreds if not thousands of similar opportunities in every corner of our community. Why can't we endow funds to eradicate the most pressing issues facing the Black community? We can! Yes, we can! We can if we hear the call to action.

CHAPTER TWELVE
ENDOWING THE CAUSE

What if, right here in the world's leading purveyor of capitalism, Black people combined their capitalistic skill and their love for the Black community to change the course of our history? What if Black businesses everywhere committed to profiting with a purpose? What if the Black community followed the model of the finest private universities in the world and created an endowment so large that we could solve any problem for which money could be a solution? Think of the impact we could have.

Imagine if we were not content with small victories, with purposeful profit just here and there. Imagine instead the presence of millions of companies large and small committed to converting profits to Black community investment and Black community investment to Black community solutions. Imagine our nation's economic landscape dotted with such like-minded companies so numerous that they could not be plotted on a map without covering every inch of our great nation's terrain. What if we as Black consumers and Black business owners wholeheartedly embraced the dual objective of making profit and investing said profit with purpose? What if we agreed that the end game was not a series of small victories, a win here and a win there, but impact so large that it stacked to the ceiling? This would be a nice start, but would not yet be endowing the cause.

The Black Endowment Company

What if these purposefully profitable companies assumed a central role in the growth and prosperity of the Black community? Just as the tithing parishioner is the lifeblood of the Black church, what if these Black Endowment Companies became the lifeblood of the Black community? What if these Black Endowment Companies opted to set aside "x" percent of their annual revenue to contribute to a Black Endowment Fund with which the Black community would rebuild itself? Black Endowment Companies would be of every size, every age, and from every industry but would unite around a common purpose, the desire to reinvest in our community in a tangible way. In exchange for allowing an annual certification by a Black-owned accounting firm, of course, a company would have the right to call itself a "Black Endowment Company." Those consumers who value supporting the Black community would know that, through their purchases, they would not simply be supporting a single member of the Black community but the Black community as a whole. We would have our best outlet ever to truly reinvest in our community. Imagine what we would do with the pent-up demand among Blacks for investing in the Black community. If we are as good as our word and our often stated desire to re-invest in the Black community, a company merely holding the designation "Black Endowment Company" would dramatically improve its fortunes. And this would be a step in the right direction, but would not yet be endowing the cause.

The Black Endowment Company structure would not only facilitate the desire to use Black-earned dollars to support Black-owned business, but it would actually create more Black-earned dollars and more Black-owned businesses. According to the report issued by the *Target Market News* entitled The Buying Power of Black America 2007, Blacks had $744 billion to spend in 2006. However, some estimates suggest only 5 percent of these available dollars are being spent annually with Black-owned businesses. If we were to double our spending with Black businesses, participating Black Endowment Companies, and those companies were to contribute 10 percent of the increased revenue to a Black endowment fund, we would start with about $4 billion to invest back into the community. Four billion dollars is not a trivial amount with which to start to address our greatest needs. At this point, we'd be on to something, but would not yet be endowing the cause.

What if the Black Endowment Fund planted its first seeds in our education system? The fund would employ the best of our collective resources to ensure that our tomorrow is brighter than our today. We are in extreme peril of suffering through a hellish tomorrow due to the rate at which are children are not being educated today. A Black community in which nearly half of our high school-aged students do not graduate high school cannot be a successful Black community and may not be a sustainable Black community. What if we planted the first seeds of the fund to determine why we cannot educate our children and to reverse this trend immediately?

Some scholars say that the issue with our schools is on the "supply side," not enough teachers per student, not enough learning resources, not enough of the money spent on learning versus securing the school buildings and repairing them. The Black Endowment Fund would begin to address this issue. Other scholars suggest that the problem lies with the "demand side" of the equation. Our students do not "demand" the education because they cannot make the link in their minds between today's education and tomorrow's success. Our students wrongly feel that their station in life is not something that education can impact. To their detriment and ours, they have not been exposed to the millions of Black stories in which one generation of education changed the destiny of several generations to follow. We will speak into the hearts and minds of these young people to help them understand that their education is their salvation and ours. This would be fantastic progress, but would not yet be endowing the cause.

I know we could count upon our most successful Blacks to create visibility to the Black Endowment Fund and ensure its success. What if Dr.

William H. Cosby led the development of a curriculum that would capture the hearts and minds of our young Black students? In addition to the foundational building blocks of reading, writing, and arithmetic, what if this curriculum included an Oprah Winfrey School of Business or a Denzel Washington Drama School or a Stevie Wonder School of Music. Maybe Michael Jordan could be the Dean of Athletics emeritus. Maybe we would even have a Spike Lee School of Cinematography or a General Colin Powell School of Foreign Policy or a Toni Morrison School of Literature.

The list of "Who's Who in Black America" in most cases would also make the Who's Who in America list as well. We have so many ultra-talented people in the Black community that I know we could find a way to have our children benefit from their talents. I imagine any "demand side" issues we had would quickly fall away when we fully engaged our brightest lights in the process.

What if these schools became private entities, professionally operated providers of world-class education? Would there be room to create partnerships with local Black-owned janitorial services, foodservice distributors, groundskeepers, book publishers, and other businesses with which a school must contract to operate? Would there be an opportunity to uplift an entire community through the improvement of its schools? You know the answer. At the point we start saving communities we would have the end in sight, but would not yet be endowing the cause.

What if this Black Endowment Fund, like the funds at private universities, became a business unto itself? What if it was making its own money while those funds were waiting to be invested in our future? Perhaps John Rogers, founder of Ariel Capital, the largest Black-owned investment company in the nation, would see to that. Perhaps under the leadership of Mr. Rogers, the fund would not only be used to bolster our schools, but would serve as venture capital for would-be entrepreneurs as well. Maybe an economic think tank would emerge to solve the conundrum that causes the owners of the most important businesses a community needs to thrive to avoid operating in predominately Black neighborhoods.

If it is true that it is easier to find a gun than a tomato in some predominately Black neighborhoods, then why aren't there more grocery stores where Black people live? Perhaps the answer to this conundrum is a Black grocery store in every Black neighborhood proving that we can support profitable big-box businesses in these areas. What if we planted more entrepreneurial seeds in our communities and created enough businesses to support all of the basic demands of the residents of those communities? What if, as in more affluent communities, the residents did not have to leave the community to get their basic needs met? Would this create even more jobs and more economic stability for the community? Again, you know the answer. At this point, we would be almost home.

What if the Black community continued to plant more seeds throughout every Black community in every state in the country and productive Black people grew in abundance? What if we planted the seeds of quality education and vibrant, bright young leaders grew in abundance? What if we planted the seeds of entrepreneurship and socially conscious Black business people grew in abundance? Most importantly, what if we planted the seeds of a reinvestment mindset into the minds of Black people? A generation of investors in the Black community would surely grow.

When we adopt this mindset, we will be investing in each other without effort, celebrating our successes without jealously, and sharing information and gaining knowledge as a matter of habit. We will have a waiting list of Black people willing to contribute, teach, help, and support our community. We will have coded in our DNA a belief in the value of investing in each other and purged ourselves of the "mythology of blingology." We will have proven the value of taking the long view in life, of planting seeds and watching them grow versus hoping to win the lottery in life. We will have created a Black community of investors who make decisions as if they expect to live forever rather than only into the middle of next week.

This would allow us to arrive at the real end game. We would be so successful in this effort that the whole process would become obsolete. The process will have worked so well that we could tear it down. It was never our intention to create a parallel society that is in America but not of America. We will have made the Black Endowment Fund obsolete because we will have proven that Black business is equal to non-Black business, no better and no worse. We will have removed the stigma that causes all consumers, Black and non-Black, to assume that a Black business is an inferior business. In fact, we will have created an environment in which all forms of "affirmative action" will be obsolete. We will no longer have to encourage or threaten businesses to hire Black talent. They will simply recognize that talent is talent and will try, as all good businesses do, to hoard the best of it. The likelihood that a Black person will be hired for any given position would be the same as the percentage of Blacks in the pool. And there would be no reason to suspect a poisoned pool. We will have realized our original Dream through our knowledge of and belief in the American dream. This would be endowing the cause.

Undoubtedly, there are challenges to the Black Endowment Fund plan that I have not yet solved. I offer this idea not as the answer, but as a starting point. The genius of capitalism does not lie in the intelligence of one person or a central group of people, but in the notion that the marketplace thrives best when millions of entities are making decisions in their best interests. Similarly, the genius in the Black community will be millions of missionaries surveying the elephant we must devour (our common problems), hauling away the piece about which they are the most passionate (our individual missions), and digesting it fully (our common solution). Hopefully this starting point will spark an inspired thought within you that will cause you to digest a piece of our elephant.

Becoming Missionaries

How could we change the Black community for the better if we unleashed thousands of people who were on a mission to make a difference? How quickly could we garner support for our causes if we used our networks to match the right people with the right resources? What would happen if we started to monetize our missions and endow our causes as do other powerful groups? Could we send the dilapidated school into extinction? Would we send the dropout rate among Black students plummeting along with teenage pregnancy rates and crime rates? Could we create a generation of mission driven entrepreneurs who would ultimately attach every product or service sold to the good it could do? Would we finally start to realize the often talked about but seldom acted upon dream of recycling more Black dollars rather being content to see them all leave the community never to return?

This is the dream we should pursue. However, we will not realize any dream until we recognize that we are the dream. The dream lives in our hearts and minds and rests in our own hands. We will never make a fundamental change within the Black community until we decide that we are the only ones who can make it happen. We can do this. All we need to make this happen is an army of missionaries. Are you ready to enlist?

CONCLUSION
IGNORE THE EVIDENCE – THE REMIX

Black people, ignore the evidence! The evidence will suggest that you can't do, can't be, can't achieve. If you do the math, you will see more Black people not doing than doing, not being than being, not achieving than achieving. You will be bombarded by evidence suggesting that you are who you are supposed to be and we the Black community are who we are supposed to be. You will see evidence that suggests that despite our relatively low flying altitude, we have reached our absolute ceiling. You will see the barriers, understand why they exist, and sometimes become overwhelmed by the enormity of our task. At the moments when you become the most overwhelmed, you must remember to ignore the evidence. You must remember to believe in your ability to succeed. You must believe in love.

You must remember that love is always worth it, no matter how many times it has hurt us in the past. You must remember that one thousand wrong loves can be completely undone and purged from memory by one right one. It only takes one love to make everything right. Love is worth believing in because love has, does, and will repeatedly change the world. You must remember that you can't prove love, but you know love is real. You must remember that the evidence is all wrong about love and, similarly, it is all wrong about a people we love, Black people. We are not destined to live in struggle as says the evidence. We can love our way to a better future. We can love our way to greatness. If we do right, we can undo any wrong. But we must ignore the evidence.

"'The Man' will never let us (fill-in the-blank)"

The evidence may suggest "The Man" is alive and well. Ignore the evidence! Some will say the evidence is obvious, as has been demonstrated time after time from slavery to Jim Crow, from Tuskegee to Katrina. It is easy for some to believe there is a force behind the curtain that exists to block our every attempt at success. Our past has determined our future. We will only enjoy the success we are allowed to have. We pulled life's short straw and there is nothing we can do about it.

Successful Black people do not believe in "The Man." They say "no pain" although on many occasions they do feel pain. "No pain" means not that pain does not exist, but that pain will not be a deterrent to success. They believe the physical pain of trying or the hardship of a temporary setback pales in comparison to the searing emotional pain of enduring failure or, worse still, the failure to try. Therefore they are willing to push through the pain.

Successful Black people say "no fear" although on many occasions they do feel fear. "No fear" means not that they have no fears, but that they love their greatness more than they fear its price. This love causes them to face their fears. They say "The Man" does not exist not because they believe that racism does not exist but because they feel that racism is irrelevant. They understand "The Man" is a voice in their own minds they must keep silent in order to be successful. In so doing, no amount of bias can stop them from achieving their missions in life. Their mission is too righteous and their passion is too strong to be defeated. Their love is stronger than any amount of hate. Therefore, in their eyes, "The Man" is dead. We can have this level of conviction as well, but we must ignore the evidence.

"To explain the failure, find the racism"

The evidence may suggest that racism is at the root of all of our failures. Ignore the evidence! Too many of us are Ph.D.s in racial math, possessing the ability to solve any racial equation no matter how complex. Just as those who believe in capitalism believe the logic behind every situation can be ascertained by "following the money," racial math Ph.D.s believe that every situation can be explained by following the racism. According to the Ph.D.s, Blacks never fail based on the strict merits of a present day situation. Whites defeat Blacks in business situations due to racism. Blacks turn on other Blacks due to racism. Blacks self-sabotage due to racism. There are not six degrees of separation but rather one or two between racism and every negative outcome a Black person has ever experienced, according to the Ph.D.s. According to the Ph.D.s, this lesson is always apparent as school is always in session. However, successful Blacks do not and never will attend this school.

Successful living is powerful living. Successful Black people know assigning blame also means giving up power. Successful people are unwilling to give up the power over their own lives. They believe, not selectively but categorically, that they can and do control their future. They are unwilling to concede that their fate was foretold by their ethnicity. They refuse to believe that the millions of Black people who have had success in America's history did so because some mighty and malevolent force simply allowed it. They do not believe our success was simply a cosmic clerical error, something that simply slipped through the cracks. Successful Black people believe success is earned and they have the ability and the right to earn it. They spend no time at all trying to figure out how they were defeated by an unseen force. Instead, they plan for victory.

There is no value for us in getting advanced degrees in racial math. We must get our undergraduate degree in winning rather than explaining and then excusing our losses. We must get our master's degree in unrigging rigged games rather than complaining that the game we are playing is not fair. We must get our Ph.D.s in being so skillful in our areas of expertise and so committed to our missions that we evade traps before the competition even thinks to set them. We must get an education in something, anything, other than the outdated, backward-looking science of racial math. We can bury this archaic science, but first we must ignore the evidence.

"Only real Blacks can join us in the struggle"

The evidence may suggest that finding the "double agents" within the Black community is important work. Ignore the evidence! Too many of us are engaged in an endless search for "double agent" Blacks to expose and excommunicate from the Black community. However, we must realize this work is for people who are not busy enough striving, so idle they have time to mind someone else's business rather than their own. Once we get busy with our own missions, we will find no time to inspect the musical tastes, hobbies, or sartorial style of our peers. When we are focused enough on success, we will recognize that proper English is the language of commerce, not the voice of treason, and education is an indispensable tool, not a worthless distraction. Once we get busy enough, we will all be doing as successful Black people do.

Successful Black people have abandoned wasting any time determining which Blacks are "real" by last century's standard. They know that allies can change but interests stay constant. It is always in our interest to create an environment in which Blacks can succeed to the level of our skill and our will. However, it is not a given which people or political parties will be our best partners as we pursue our interests. Therefore, we cannot include in our definition of "real" an affiliation to a specific person or political party. In fact, the people who will lead the Black community to future greatness know that the whole concept of determining who is "real" is a fool's errand that serves to prevent success, not enable it. Separating fake Blacks from real ones based upon some dubious set of criteria is no different morally than others suggesting Black people are not "real Americans" due to the color of their skin. Both exercises are wrong-headed and not worthy of the time of successful people. We can have this clarity of understanding, but we must ignore the evidence.

"You know how Black folks are"

The evidence may suggest that Blacks carry insurmountable historical burdens and thus the bar for our achievement should be lower. Ignore the evidence! We must reject this notion out of hand. We are not an inferior people and therefore we do not need anyone to dumb down the measures of success for us. We are the masters of our fate, the captains of our own destiny. We can lay down the pipe. We can be mothers and fathers to our children. We can stop our babies from having babies. We can educate ourselves well enough to excel in a global economy. We can stop killing each other. Any suggestion to the contrary is foolish, no matter who makes it. We will not give anyone the satisfaction of believing we are inferior by agreeing with them. Therefore we will not excuse or condone any behavior that does not promote our success.

You know how Black folks are? Yes, I know how Black folks are. Black folks are intelligent, resilient, resourceful, thoughtful, caring, loving, and successful. That's how Black folks are. We cannot accept any suggestion to the contrary no matter who makes it. We must resist any and every temptation to grade ourselves on a curve. If can always keep our remarkable legacy of success front of mind, we always remember that success is our birthright. This is the evidence upon which we should focus.

An Audaciously Hopeful New World

The Black community has a right to be audacious. Our failure was not foretold by our past. Our victory was foretold. We have inherited a legacy of striving, thriving, and overcoming. We have already beaten the odds millions of times. We have already demonstrated immeasurable strength and intestinal fortitude. We are of a people whose spirit is not simply strong, or stronger than strong, but invincible. We have earned the right to be audacious. We should be audaciously hopeful as we consider our future.

With this audacious hope, we will find the courage to love. We will find the courage to love ourselves enough to demand success and expect nothing less. With this audacious hope, we will find the courage to love the Black community enough to trust each other with our fates. We will find the courage to open up to each other in collaboration and strive for the biggest prizes together rather than "playing small" as individuals. We will find the courage to encourage and celebrate each other's successes. With this audacious hope, we will love our future generations enough to free our own minds. We will find the courage to abandon retrospective thinking and to risk "letting 'The Man' off the hook" to speak openly about our problems. We will find the courage to do right rather than to be right. We will find the courage to spit out the venom we are harboring regarding the legacy of slavery and Jim Crow before it kills us. We may have a right to a million grievances, but not one of them will make us more successful tomorrow. We will find the courage to break free from our chains for the final time. And when we do so, we will have laid down our hate in favor of love. We will find the courage to love.

The Black community, as Dr. King said, must sign its own emancipation proclamation. We cannot wait for anyone else to make the wrongs right. If we desire true freedom, we have to make it so. As Barack Obama said, we must embrace the audacity of hope. We must choose to believe that wildly better days are ahead. We must expect this future for ourselves, and then do the hard work to make it so. We must fulfill our obligation to the next generation of Black people. We must gift them an inheritance as significant as the one we were left. We must author our own version of Brown v. Board of Education, our own Civil Rights Act.

The gift that we will give ourselves, our people, and our children is the gift of love. If we love enough, Black people will not simply be successful, but our impact on the world will be everlasting. Love is our answer. Love is the only answer. Therefore, this is my *Love Letter to Black People.*

REFERENCES

Books / Articles

Frankin, John Hope and Alfred A. Moss, Jr. From Slavery to Freedom: A History of African Americans, Seventh Edition. New York: Alfred A. Knopf, 1994.

Janssen, Sarah (Editor). The World Almanac and Book of Facts 2008. New York: World Almanac Books, 2007.

Seligman, M.E.P. Helplessness: On Depression, Development, and Death. San Francisco: W.H. Freeman, 1975.

Williamson, Marianne. A Return to Love: Reflections on the Principles of "A Course in Miracles. New York: Harper Paperbacks, 1996.

Newspaper

Banaji, Mahzarin. "What are the costs of being black?" The Atlanta Journal-Constitution 6 Apr. 2008: E3.

Newspaper Article on the Internet

Morin, Richard. "The Name is No Game." The Washington Post. 27 Mar 2005: B05. The Washington Post Company. 18 July 2008. http://www.washingtonpost.com/wp-dyn/articles/A2524-2005Mar26.html

Web sites

Baram, Marcus. "The Sissyness of Hope." 7 Mar. 2008. ABCNews.com. 22 July 2008. http://abcnews.go.com/Politics/Story?id=4410684&page=1

"Bill Cosby: Address at the NAACP on the 50th Anniversary of Brown v. Board of Education." n.d. AmericanRhetoric.com. 18 July 2008. http://www.americanrhetoric.com/speeches/billcosbypoundcakespeech.htm

Dawidziak, Mark. "Analysis: Barack Obama speech on race a challenge for TV pundits." 18 Mar. 2008. Cleveland.com. 19 June 2008. http://blog.cleveland.com/openers/2008/03/analysis_barack_obama_speech_o.html

"Education pays..." n.d. Bureau of Labor Statistics. 18 July 2008. http://www.bls.gov/emp/emptab7.htm

"Food From the 'Hood." n.d. Corporation for Educational Radio and Television. 20 July 2008. http://www.certnyc.org/ffth.html

Harvard Law School Library Nuremberg Trials Project. N.d. 10 July 2008. http://nuremberg.law.harvard.edu/php/docs_swi.php?DI=1&text=overview

"HIV / AIDS." n.d. The Henry J. Kaiser Family Foundation. 19 July 2008. http://www.kff.org/hivaids/upload/3029-071.pdf

"Homicide Trends in the United States." n.d. Bureau of Justice Statistics. 18 July 2008. http://www.ojp.usdoj.gov/bjs/homicide/race.htm

"How to Keep a Black Man Down." N.d. AfricanAmericanImage.com. 17 July 2008. http://www.africanamericanimages.com/aai/willie%20Lynch.htm

"Keynote Address at the 2004 Democratic National Convention." n.d. BarackObama.com. 19 June 2008. http://www.barackobama.com/2004/07/27/keynote_address_at_the_2004_de.php

Mundell, E.J. "U.S. Blacks Seek Answers to AIDS Epidemic." 1 Dec. 2007. SexualHealth.com. 19 July 2008. http://sexualhealth.e-healthsource.com/?p=news1&id=536386

Potter, Jerry. "Tiger's father Earl Woods dies at 74." 4 May 2006. USAToday.com. 6 Aug. 2008. http://www.usatoday.com/sports/golf/pga/2006-05-03-earl-woods-obit_x.htm

"Research Ethics: The Tuskegee Syphilis Study." N.d. TuskegeeUniversity.edu. 10 July 2008. http://www.tuskegee.edu/Global/Story.asp?s=1207598 (10 July 2008)

"Selling out." n.d. Wikipedia.org. 1 August 2008. http://en.wikipedia.org/wiki/Selling_out

"Stop Snitching." 22 Apr. 2007. 60Minutes.com. 18 July 2008. http://60minutes.yahoo.com/segment/60/stop_snitching

"The 2008 HHS Poverty Guidelines." n.d. United States Department of Health & Human Services. 18 July 2008. http://aspe.hhs.gov/poverty/08Poverty.shtml

The Associated Press. "Georgia Rep. Who Endorsed Clinton Faces Rare Primary Challenge." 10 July 2008. FoxNews.com. 15 July 2008. http://elections.foxnews.com/2008/07/10/georgia-rep-who-endorsed-clinton-faces-rare-primary-challenge

"The Buying Power of Black America 2007." n.d. Target Market News: The Black Consumer Market Authority. 28 July 2008. http://www.targetmarketnews.com/BuyingPower05.htm

"The State of Black America 2008: In the Black Woman's Voice." n.d. National Urban League. 5 April 2008. blications/SOBA/Executive%20Summary/2008SOBAEXCSUMMARY.pdf

ARE YOU SUCCESS MINDED?

IF SO, JOIN THE
SUCCESS MINDED AFRICAN AMERICANS NETWORKING GROUP AT:

http://successminded.ning.com

OR ON LINKEDIN AT:

http://www.linkedin.com/e/gis/115994

OR ON THE BRIAN McCLELLAN WEB SITE AT:

http://www.bamstrong.com